# THE MILAN SEMINAR

# The History of Psychoanalysis Series

*Professor Brett Kahr and Professor Peter L. Rudnytsky (Series Editors)*
Published and distributed by Karnac Books

## Other titles in the Series

# THE MILAN SEMINAR

## Clinical Applications of Attachment Theory

*John Bowlby, edited by*
*Marco Bacciagaluppi*

Routledge
Taylor & Francis Group

LONDON AND NEW YORK

First published 2013 by
Karnac Books Ltd.

Published 2018 by Routledge
2 Park Square, Milton Park, Abingdon, Oxon OX14 4RN
711 Third Avenue, New York, NY 10017, USA

*Routledge is an imprint of the Taylor & Francis Group, an informa business*

British Library Cataloguing in Publication Data

A C.I.P. for this book is available from the British Library

ISBN 9781780491677 (pbk)


Edited, designed and produced by The Studio Publishing Services Ltd
www.publishingservicesuk.co.uk
e-mail: studio@publishingservicesuk.co.uk

# CONTENTS

# ACKNOWLEDGEMENTS

The editor is very grateful to Sir Richard Bowlby for allowing him to quote from his correspondence with John Bowlby and for granting permission to publish the material by John Bowlby in the seminar.

He thanks his son Claudio for having prepared a CD with excerpts from the seminar.

His thanks are due to Claudia Ferrandes for permission to make use of the audio recording of the seminar.

He is also grateful to his computer expert Carlos Baldovino for his indispensable technical assistance.

# ABOUT THE EDITOR AND CONTRIBUTORS

**Germana Agnetti** graduated at the University of Milan Medical School and then received postgraduate training in Psychiatry and Medical Psychology at the University of Milan. After a Kleinian analysis, she also trained in systemic family therapy in Milan and Palo Alto (USA). She has held positions in psychiatry at the University of Calgary (Canada), at the Eastern Metropolitan Psychiatric Services in Melbourne (Australia), and at the Department of Mental Health of Niguarda Hospital Trust, Milan. She is currently Co-director, IRIS Postgraduate School of Psychotherapy, Milan. She is on the Board of Directors of the World Association for Psychosocial Rehabilitation and is a Member of the Italian Society for Systems Research and Therapy.

**Marco Bacciagaluppi** graduated at the University of Milan Medical School and then received postgraduate training in genetics and radiobiology at the Department of Genetics of the University of Pavia, in psychiatry at the Department of Psychiatry of the University of Milan and at New York Medical College, and in sociology at the New School for Social Research, New York. After psycho-analytic training, since 1999 he has co-operated in organising thirteen Joint Meetings between the American Academy of Psychoanalysis and Dynamic Psychiatry (AAPDP) and the Organizzazione di Psicoanalisti Italiani – Federazione e Registro (OPIFER). He is a Fellow of AAPDP, Founding President of OPIFER, Honorary Member of the International Erich Fromm Society (IEFS), Member of the World Psychiatric Association (WPA) Section on Psychotherapy, and Member of the Associazione Culturale Sándor Ferenczi (ACSF). He has just published *Paradigms in Psychoanalysis* (Bacciagaluppi, 2012).

**Angelo Barbato** graduated at the University of Palermo Medical School and then received postgraduate training in psychiatry at the University of Milan and in psychiatric epidemiology at the Université Pierre et Marie Curie, Paris. After a Kleinian analysis, he trained in group psychotherapy and psychoeducational family therapy in Milan. He has held positions in psychiatry at the Eastern Metropolitan Psychiatric Services in Melbourne (Australia) and at the Department of Mental Health of the Salvini Hospital Trust, Garbagnate, Milan. He is currently Co-director, IRIS Postgraduate School of Psychotherapy, Milan, and Senior Scientist, Laboratory of Epidemiology and Social Psychiatry, Mario Negri Institute, Milan. He is Past President, World Association for Psychosocial Rehabilitation, and Member of the Italian Society of Psychiatric Epidemiology, of the Association of European Psychiatrists, and of the Society for Psychotherapy Research.

**John Bowlby** (1907–1990) studied medicine and psychology in Cambridge, then completed his medical training in London, trained in psychiatry at the Maudsley Hospital and in psychoanalysis with Joan Riviere and Melanie Klein, with a special emphasis on children. He was a life-long member of the British Psychoanalytical Society, where he belonged to the Middle Group, now known as the Independent Group. Before the Second World War, he published a book on aggressiveness and war with his friend Evan Durbin. After his early work on homeless children for the World Health Organisation (WHO), he developed attachment theory in the trilogy of *Attachment, Separation and Loss*, which was published over a twelve-year period. The theory is based on ethology and evolutionary theory, but also has a strong emphasis on interpersonal relations, family dynamics, and cognitive mechanisms. He worked for many years at the Tavistock Clinic, with the support of American foundations, and taught and lectured widely in the United States. His last book was a biography of Charles Darwin.

**Claudia Ferrandes**, after having received her high-school certificate as a dietician, graduated in hospital dietotherapy and clinical nutrition at the University of Pavia (1975), then studied Philosophy at the University of Milan (1982–1985). She has worked as a dietician at the Ospedale San Carlo Borromeo in Milan (1972–1992) where, in the team of Giuseppe d'Amico, she developed the first diet in Italy for nephro-pathic patients undergoing haemodialysis. She then specialised further in cognitive–behavioural psychotherapy of eating disorders with Riccardo Dalle Grave (1990–2002). In 2002–2005, she took part in the Italian Core Training in Intensive Experiential–Dynamic Psychotherapy, directed by Ferruccio Osimo. She specialises in the psycho-nutritional treatment of patients with eating disorders.

**Emilia Fumagalli** graduated in Philosophy and specialised in Psychology at the University of Milan. She received postgraduate training in psychodynamic psychotherapy and systemic family ther-apy, and also trained at the Tavistock Clinic. After working as a psychologist and teaching in several Italian public institutions, she has been Chief of Psychology at the Ospedale Niguarda Cà Granda of Milan since July 2009. Her work in a large public hospital enables her not only to evaluate but also to give help, at an individual and family level, to inpatients and outpatients with severe somatic conditions. She is the author of several papers on therapeutic models and the therapeutic process. She has a special concern for problems connected with mental illness.

**Ferruccio Osimo** graduated in Medicine from the University of Padova and specialised in Psychiatry at the University of Milan. He trained in dynamic psychotherapy at the Tavistock Clinic in London (1981–1983), where he carried out in-depth process and outcome clinical studies, co-authoring with David Malan the book *Psychodynamics, Training, and Outcome in Brief Psychotherapy* (1992). He attended Habib Davanloo's core training in intensive short-term dynamic psychotherapy in Geneva (1988–1991), and took part in the Short-Term Dynamic Psychotherapy Research Program directed by Leigh McCullough at Harvard Medical School (1997). He was the first President (2001–2007) of the International Experiential Dynamic Therapy Association, and is the President of the Italian EDT Association. He is a Fellow of the American Academy of Psychoanalysis and Dynamic Psychiatry

(AAPDP) and Member of the Organizzazione di Psicoanalisti Italiani – Federazione e Registro (OPIFER). He runs the Italian, UK, and Israeli advanced training programmes in IE-DP. He lives in Milan and teaches at the School of Psychiatry of the University. His clinical work has been presented internationally. His latest book is *Theory and Practice of Experiential Dynamic Psychotherapy* (Osimo & Stein, 2012).

**Leopolda Pelizzaro** graduated in Psychology at the University of Padova. From 1973 to 1976 she had a scholarship with the aim of establishing a connection between the Faculties of Psychology and Medicine, and in 1975 she obtained a scholarship at UCLA. She is a psycho-oncologist and an Associate Member of SPI (Società Psico-analitica Italiana). She worked for thirty-five years at the Fatebene-fratelli Hospital of Milan with psychotic and oncological patients. In 2000 she founded the psychological service at the hospice of the hospital, in order to help the families of terminal patients deal with the prospect of loss. She has conducted Balint groups at the Milan Polyclinic with the medical and paramedical staff that dealt with organ transplants. She has been a supervisor at the School of Psychotherapy of Imagination. At present she works as a psycho-analyst.

# SERIES EDITOR'S FOREWORD

For more than sixty years, Edward John Mostyn Bowlby devoted his life to the understanding of children. As a physician, as a child psychiatrist, as a psychoanalyst, as a research scientist, and as a public educator, Bowlby did more than perhaps any other mental health professional since Sigmund Freud to explore the impact of early traumatic experiences of deprivation, loss, abuse, and misattunement on the growing infant, investigating the ways in which abandonment, separation, and family secrets contribute to psychopathology in later life. Through his books, his essays, and his lectures, Bowlby helped to create a new accent in psychology—attachment theory—and in doing so, he effected a veritable paradigm shift in our field. As the American psychoanalyst Dr Jules Bemporad once remarked, "He was the last of the giants".

Dr Marco Bacciagaluppi, the distinguished Italian psychiatrist, psychoanalyst, and attachment scholar, has bequeathed to us a remarkable gift. He has edited and introduced the transcript of Bowlby's hitherto unpublished seminar held in 1985, in Milan. An early contributor to the field of Bowlby scholarship, Bacciagaluppi has not only prepared a beautifully readable text of Bowlby's visit with Italian colleagues, but he has also shared his extensive correspondence with Bowlby over many years, allowing us a detailed glimpse of Bowlby, both in public and in private. As Kate White, Editor of the journal *Attachment: New Directions in Psychotherapy and Relational Psychoanalysis*, has observed in her warm and gracious Foreword to this book, Bacciagaluppi has brought Bowlby back to life, and thus, he has given us a precious keepsake.

Reading the transcript of Bowlby's seminar, contemporary readers have the opportunity of witnessing not only Bowlby's finely tuned clinical skills, but also of enjoying Bowlby as a critic of orthodox psychoanalysis. In many respects, this seminar constitutes a veritable master class on modern, relational, attachment-orientated approaches to psychoanalytical work as Bowlby encourages his audience to move beyond the confines of the transference interpretation—useful though that might be—to a more dynamic conversation between two participants who share a curiosity about the world of the client. One also enjoys Bowlby helping colleagues to appreciate the role of real-life trauma, a crucial antidote to his own orthodox Kleinian training, which focused predominantly on unconscious phantasy. As Bowlby notes in this Milan seminar, "I think it's vital that we respect the real-life experiences which patients report."

Bowlby had the courage of his convictions, but he never proselytised. When, on one occasion, he disagreed with a colleague who held, perhaps, more antiquated views, Bowlby responded, quite simply and quite charmingly, "I think you are wearing a pair of spectacles which are different from mine." Thanks to the impressive scholarly work of Marco Bacciagaluppi, and to the fine clinical contributions from several of his eminent Italian colleagues, we now have a precious opportunity to look through Bowlby's spectacles, and to see the world as he did.

Professor Brett Kahr
Co-Editor, History of Psychoanalysis Series

# FOREWORD

I think it's vital that we respect the real-life experiences which patients report. I think it's vital that we accept them as likely to be valid. But we also have to be accepting, in the sense of providing the patient with a secure base. We have to be the patient's attachment figure. Perhaps I can give an analogy. In so far as patients are telling us about painful, frightening experiences, we have to be a companion who gives them courage. (Bowlby, 1985, Milan Seminar)

Marco Bacciagaluppi, as editor of this book, has gathered together some remarkable historical material, bringing to life John Bowlby's contribution to a seminar held in Milan in 1985, nearly thirty years ago. In addition, there is Bacciagaluppi's correspondence with John Bowlby, and Ferruccio Osimo presents a section on the brief therapy approach of experiential dynamic therapy (EDT) and how this is informed by attachment theory.

It is a remarkable and moving story that Marco Bacciagaluppi has brought to us, in which we find new and textured accounts of John Bowlby's application of his own theory to the clinical work of his Italian colleagues. It is similar to being at a live supervision event, with Bowlby as the supervisor, bringing his razor-sharp insight and his distinctive and humane approach to such issues as the efficacy of telephone sessions and the length and frequency of therapeutic sessions with people with very troubled attachment histories. His clarity of thinking, for example, around—in his view outdated—concepts of "regression" and "dependency", are freshly understood within the theoretical breadth and depth of attachment theory.

Bacciagaluppi has made, and continues to make, a remarkable contribution to the integration and the discovery of common ground between different theoreticians. His pioneering work was to bring together the work of John Bowlby and Erich Fromm to elucidate their common purpose in the pursuit of the recognition of the impact of the social environment on human emotional development, as well as the centrality of love for us as humans. It was in this context that, in 1994, The Bowlby Centre invited Marco to give a presentation about the links between Bowlby, attachment theory, and Fromm. We recognised his talent for integration and his spirit of exploration, which have been a hallmark of his career.

What is clear from Marco's introduction to this book, where we gain a privileged insight into their correspondence, is the way Bowlby was open to discussing and sharing his work with colleagues the world over, and in this way disseminating his ideas across disciplines and across continents.

In reading these letters and transcriptions of John Bowlby's words, I am reminded of the experience we might have of discovering a hidden treasure trove of letters or keepsakes belonging to someone we have loved who has died, and having a "heart-leap" moment as we, for a while, are transported into a world where they are once more alive and we have access to their wisdom once more . . . It was like that for me as I read these papers, touched to the core by Bowlby's brilliance, clarity, and humanity.

What a project Marco and his contributors have pulled off: it is a riveting read whether you are a historian or a clinician. To have these primary sources is gold dust. To have the story of these colleagues coming together at a particular moment in time in 1985 is quite magical. I found the background account of the Milan Seminar so interesting, as it painted the picture of the confluence of ideas within the social and political context of that time, Bowlby's revolution in attachment theory finding an echo with the Italian anti-psychiatry movement and the flowering of systems thinking with its radical application to family therapy, still in its infancy.

To conclude, we are indebted to Marco and his colleagues for their vision and meticulous attention to detail in bringing to life a remarkable event, which has had a long-lasting influence on the development of an attachment-informed and relationally inspired psychotherapy in Italy and which now is available to us all to learn from and appreciate.

Kate White
Editor of *Attachment: New Directions in Psychotherapy and Relational Psychoanalysis*, Series Editor of *The John Bowlby Memorial Conference Monographs*, and Training Therapist and former Chair of the Clinical Training Committee at The Bowlby Centre

# Introduction and correspondence

*Marco Bacciagaluppi*

I must first of all justify my position as editor of a seminar at which I was not present because of another engagement elsewhere. However, I was much involved in all other respects. I was a great admirer of Bowlby from the very beginning, and had read the three books of his trilogy as soon as they were published, starting in 1969. My wife immediately applied attachment theory when, the next year, our first-born boy, aged five, had to be hospitalised, and she insisted on "rooming in"—a very uncommon practice in those days, especially in Italy. In 2012, I published a book, *Paradigms in Psychoanalysis* (Bacciagaluppi, 2012), in which there is a special emphasis on Bowlby. By editing the seminar, I am trying to compensate for my absence.

This introduction is divided into four parts: my correspondence with Bowlby, the seminar, my own comments on the seminar, and further contributions to this book.

## My correspondence with Bowlby

In addition to the seminar, readers might be interested in further unpublished material from my correspondence with Bowlby, which covers a span of eight years, from 1982 to 1990, the year he died. Since we cited many authors in our exchange, this explains the long list of references at the end of this Introduction. My editorial comments within the letters are in square brackets. Our language is not always gender neutral, as was usual at the time. Bowlby explicitly mentions this subject in a footnote on p. 3 of *A Secure Base* (Bowlby, 1988b): "Throughout this book the child is referred to as masculine in order to avoid clumsy constructions".

My first extant letter to Bowlby is dated 31st March 1982, but it refers to earlier contacts that I did not find in my records. "In 1979 I unfortunately missed an opportunity of meeting you in London [because my younger boy had developed measles; instead, I met in London Dorothy Heard, who had applied attachment theory to family therapy (Heard, 1978)]." In this first letter, I enclosed a paper I had written with my wife on "The relevance of ethology to interpersonal psychodynamics and to wider social issues" (Bacciagaluppi & Bacciagaluppi-Mazza, 1982a).

> It gives my wife and me great pleasure to send you the reprint of a paper which is basically inspired by your work. It is a preliminary and, we hope, not totally undeserving attempt to integrate your ethological approach with our clinical work in psychoanalysis, which is based on the American interpersonal–cultural school. We also try to point out the great fruitfulness of your approach in connection with wider issues. In the future, we plan to study more systematically the impact of interpersonal factors on innate behavioural systems.

In his reply of the 26th April, Bowlby objected, correctly, to our having connected his work to that of Margaret Mahler (Mahler, Pine, & Bergman, 1975). He wrote,

> Many thanks for sending me a copy of your recent paper. I am naturally very glad to know that you are finding my ideas useful in your theoretical and clinical work. Although Margaret Mahler has been concerned with the same problems that I have and some of our clinical practices are not dissimilar, the theories we have proposed I believe to be much more different than you suppose. Mahler's theories are placed within the traditional framework of phases of development, fixation and regression. A key concept here is that psychological states which in later life are judged pathological are believed to

be reflections of psychological states of infancy that are normal phases of development. By contrast, my theories are placed within the framework of developmental biology, in which the key notion is that of developmental pathway (see the final chapter of Volume 2). Let me illustrate by reference to Mahler's concept of an autistic phase to which, you suggest, the reaction of detachment during separation may be considered as a defensive regression. First, Mahler's concept of an autistic phase is certainly not supported by any of the recent work on babies, e.g. by Daniel Stern [here Bowlby is referring to one or several of Stern's early papers; his main work, in which Bowlby is often cited, appeared in 1985], which show unmistakeably that the youngest babies are not only able to interact with mother in a social way but enjoy doing so. Thus, I believe the notion of an autistic phase to be quite mistaken. Secondly, I believe the detachment response to be a pathological deviation in development of a kind in no way characteristic of normal development. These criticisms of Mahler's theories are presented more fully by Milton Klein in a recent article in the Journal of Contemporary Psychoanalysis [actually, in *Psychoanalysis and Contemporary Thought*: Klein, 1981]. There is a great deal in the rest of your paper with which I find myself in general agreement. It is very heartening to find so many analysts moving in the same direction.

In my reply of the 31st May, I said,

We realized, of course, that Mahler works in a different frame of reference, but when we tried to integrate her contributions with yours, we evidently got caught in some residual traditional thinking of our own. We shall certainly bear your remarks in mind in our future work.

I then ask what other analysts were moving in the same direction as he.

To our knowledge, there are not many in the American interpersonal–cultural school, to which we belong. One was the late David Schecter [1978], whom we quote repeatedly in our paper. To be informed of the work of these other analysts could be of great help for our further work. We would like to study systematically in our clinical material the interference of interpersonal factors with innate patterns of behaviour.

I enclosed a memorial article on Silvano Arieti (Bacciagaluppi & Bacciagaluppi Mazza, 1982b).

He was our teacher in New York in 1963–64, and we later translated most of his books into Italian. The memorial article was published originally in Italian. Unfortunately, several passages were omitted by the American editor. I think you might be particularly interested in the following one: 'Though it is true that the patient uses primitive cognitive mechanisms which distort his perceptions, he also does so in response to environmental cues. For instance, if the patient has a split image of the mother, this also occurs because the mother, in order to maintain a good self-image in her own eyes and in those of others, often presents the patient with a split image of herself. . . . In a wider context, the evolutionary approach is possibly one of the aspects of Arieti's work most worthy of development. All his work is firmly rooted in the theory of evolution. As regards cognitive mechanisms, Arieti suggests, for example, that the ontogenetic evolution from image to paleosymbol to symbol also reflects a phylogenetic evolution. . . . In the field of affect Arieti likewise suggests that an evolution of emotions has taken place, and from this point of view he classifies them in three orders. In particular, in a fine chapter of his book on depression [Arieti & Bemporad, 1978], he discusses the possible survival value of sadness.

Bowlby (1974) had contributed a chapter to Arieti's *American Handbook of Psychiatry*, and Arieti, in turn, expresses high regard for Bowlby in a book of his:

Bowlby considers this attachment of the child for the mother the basis for all future attachments, that is, of all future loves. . . . We, the authors of this book, believe that attachment is an important and essential part of filial love and any subsequent love. (Arieti & Arieti, 1977, p. 25)

Bowlby answered on the 24th June. "The omitted passage which you include in your letter is most interesting, especially the point about the mother presenting a split-image of herself to the patient." In reply to my query, he says, "As regards other analysts who are interested in the approach we share, I must admit they are still rather few in number". He then lists three American analysts: Mardi Horowitz (1979), John Gedo (1979) and Emanuel Peterfreund (1983) (this book was forthcoming).

Two others who have been influential in infancy research are Lou Sander of Boston [e.g., Sander, 1977] and Daniel Stern of New York [already discussed above]. In addition, there are a few newly qualified analysts who have yet to make their mark. Whatever the discipline, radical changes in conceptual framework always take a generation or more to achieve. So we have to be patient.

Shortly after, Peterfreund's major work appeared, with many references to Bowlby.

Of course, I promptly ordered these books.

In another letter, of the 22nd September, I asked his opinion on Oedipal problems.

After many misgivings, due to the magnitude of the task, I have started to write a paper in which I try to integrate oedipal and preoedipal problems from an ethological point of view. It is possible, as Freud maintained, that in our evolution an overlap of sexual maturation and dependency occurred. But in that case, we may also expect appropriate parental responses to have evolved. The Oedipus complex, as a pathological structure, may be due to later cultural developments which interfered with these appropriate responses. If this is a development typical of our species, we could not of course rely so much on ethological material, but psychoanalytic data could be reformulated and utilized. You have not addressed this problem yourself, as far as I am aware. The situations you have investigated are typically dyadic, but your concept of the subsidiary attachment figure could represent the transition to the oedipal triadic situation.

On the 13th October, Bowlby answered,

I am afraid I am in no position to assist you in your attempt to integrate oedipal and pre-oedipal problems with ethology. To be honest, I have never found the hypothesis of an oedipal phase very useful as an explanation either of child behaviour or of psychopathology. In so far as relations between a child and a parent become sexualized and rivalries with the other parent occur, I believe this to be due to emotional problems in the parents which lead them to use the child for their own purposes. In the healthily developing family, in which a child's principal attachment is to mother, with a subsidiary one to father, who usually also plays a major role in encouraging exploration and play, the dominant dynamics in the child are attachment and exploration, with sex playing only a very minor role, I believe. I have never given systematic attention to this issue. If it is to be done effectively, a reappraisal of the oedipal hypothesis should focus on data the hypothesis is intended to explain and consider alternative ways of explaining it. Unfortunately, this approach, central to all scientific procedure, is all too rare in the psychoanalytic literature.

I answered on the 29th November.

Your emphasis on the role of the parents' emotional problems in giving rise to oedipal problems in the child is most interpersonal, and I agree wholeheartedly. However, I think a case could be made out for the existence of an innate component as well. If, as the Harlows observed, there is an overlap of sexual maturation and dependency in rhesus monkeys, we may expect it even more in humans, in which dependency lasts so much longer. . . . Even if this extension of your approach proves unjustified, it may serve to stimulate discussion. My friend Dr. Jules Bemporad, of Harvard Medical School, who met you recently at a party in your honour given in Cambridge [MA], tells me that the paper stimulated him to reconsider all of childhood from an ethological point of view.

In a later letter of the 14th March 1983, I wrote,

After reading your third volume, I recently went back to read over again several chapters of your earlier volumes. Coming from the neo-Freudian area (a Lockean position) it is natural that my first response on reading your work should have been to your ethological viewpoint (a complementary Leibnizian position). But closer study shows other points of contact with the neo-Freudian school. (a) A strongly inter-personal approach: you constantly emphasize the importance of early experience, in contrast to the orthodox view. (b) A cognitive approach, which is especially evident in the third volume, e.g. all of Chapter 4, and p. 234, where you stress the importance of the complementary pair of models of self and parents; this aspect is especially close to Arieti's work. (c) In your ethological viewpoint there is potentially a critical theory of society; it may thus provide a base for continuing the work of Erich Fromm, and in particular for emerging from the crisis of psychoanalysis described by him. These points of contact probably explain why your work should appeal so much to neo-Freudians like Dr. Bemporad and me, and stimulate us to apply it and extend it.

Bowlby replied on the 30th March 1983:

I am sorry to have been so long in answering your letter of the 14th March, but I am only just back from a lecture tour in the United States.

Whilst in New York I addressed the Karen Horney Psychoanalytic Institute [this is when he presented "Violence in the family" on the 19th March] and also the William Alanson White Psychoanalytic Society. On both occasions a great deal of interest was shown in attachment theory, which seems now to have become established in clinical circles. As you say, the emphasis on interpersonal relationships and early experiences leads to us all having much in common.

I was hoping to meet Bowlby in London in July 1983, but in my letter of the 8th June I had to cancel my appointment owing to health problems in my family. My wife had developed a malignancy. "Health problems keep preventing me from coming to England. I really hope for better luck next year." I sent him my Oedipus paper (Bacciagaluppi, 1984) under separate cover.

You may be particularly interested in the fourth case, that of a female patient who was hospitalized during her first year of life without her mother's presence. . . . I wanted to expand on Fromm's discussion of the case of Little Hans [Fromm, 1970] and also refer to your own discussion of the case [Bowlby, 1973, pp. 284–287], but they told me the paper was already too long.

On the 6th July, Bowlby wrote,

Your overall perspective is very congenial. I am sure you are right in attributing the pathological features of Oedipal conflicts to the emotional problems that a child's parents bring to the situation, and that in the absence of parental pathology the child's conflicts are readily resolvable. I like your emphasis on the role played by the father as a subsidiary attachment figure; and also your suggestion that early maternal rejection followed by a later seductive attitude is especially pathological.

In a later letter of the 2nd August, impelled by my wife's problem, I discuss the psychodynamics of tumours. The most recent book I had on the subject was edited by Jane Goldberg (1981).

LeShan upholds a 'loss-depression' hypothesis. Cancer could thus be a special disordered variant of mourning through ill health. You yourself do not discuss these variants, but in your third volume (p. 137) you refer to a 1970 paper by Parkes. Other studies support this hypothesis. Thomas, for instance, in a prospective research at Johns Hopkins found striking similarities between those who developed cancer and those who committed suicide. We are wondering, however, if a distinction, implying another extension of your theory should not be made between two types of attachment, and therefore between two types of loss: a primary, parent–child attachment, and a later bonding between peers. If the first type of relationship was bad (what we call 'bad symbiosis' and you term 'invertion of normal parent–child relationship'), the second type will be all the more important as an indispensable, life-giving alternative. The loss of the second type of relationship (which may also be a psychological loss, a disappointment) may cause the patient to fall back onto the original bad symbiosis, giving rise to a feeling of helplessness in the face of internalized, infantile, intrusive and devouring symbiotic parents. Here, of course, we come to diverging pathways. The somatic pathway of cancer seems to pass through the immune system. In a stimulating Jungian contribution by Lockhart to Goldberg's volume it is suggested that in the breakdown of the immune system in cancer the self loses its immunity against not-self. Thus, I could add, reproducing the helplessness of the child against invasive parents. Wider issues are also involved. In the paper quoted above, Lockhart says: 'Cancer may be an inevitable price modern man pays for separating himself too far from the life of nature'. He later asks if there may be 'a connection between man's destruction, ravaging, and polluting of the earth in modern times and the increasing emergence of cancer'. This formal analogy may reveal a substantive link, consisting in an exploitative attitude towards nature which was brought about by the domestication of plants and animals, and was then extended to children within the family. Please forgive the length of this letter, which is obviously due to my present involvement in the subject. But it is also a tribute to the fruitfulness of your approach, to which we have turned once more.

## On the 28th September 1983, Bowlby replied,

Although I believe attachment theory may well be fruitful in the psychosomatic field, I think we must be cautious in making claims until we have good evidence. There is always danger of good ideas being discredited by excessive claims. The relationship of psychodynamics to tumours is a topic about which I have little knowledge, although I am aware of much interest in it. Many people have suspected that the immune system may be influenced by emotional state, but evidence seems to have been difficult to come by. I understand, however, that an article is appearing this Autumn from a group at the Mount Sinai Hospital in New York (led by Marvin Stein) on the suppression of lymphocyte stimulation following bereavement [I do not have the exact reference].

My next letter is dated the 30th November. "I quite agree that caution is called for." I raise the question of the integration of psycho-dynamic concepts into quantititative research.

One drawback of quantitative studies is that the quality of the relationship is neglected. The integration of such studies with psycho-dynamic concepts could lead to the identification of important sub-groupings. For instance, in the case of the loss of a spouse, it may be important to distinguish cases in which a transferential component is present. . . . Irrespective of the applications to cancer, this leads me back to a more general point I raised in my last letter, namely that, in addition to parent–child attachment, a later bonding between peers could be considered. Dr. Bemporad puts forth this hypothesis in a manuscript he sent me recently, titled "From attachment to affiliation" [Bemporad, 1984; Bemporad had presented this paper at the same meeting at which Bowlby presented 'Violence in the family']. This bond in turn could be a phase leading to an adult relationship between partners. An innate tendency towards a stable relationship with a partner would be of survival value in the human species. A related tendency in children may be the tendency to keep parents united. The threat of separation between parents always seems to elicit anxiety and reparative behaviour in children.

Bowlby replied on the 3rd January 1984:

I agree with you that it will be necessary to consider whether there are sub-groups which can be specified psychodynamically, in particular relationships to which a disordered relationship with parents has become transferred. I think we are still rather ignorant about the shift from a child–parent relationship to a spouse relationship. I am sure it is perfectly healthy for many components of the earlier relationship to be transferred to the new one, and that this only gives rise to trouble when the earlier relationship has been a disturbed one. As Dr. Bemporad suggests, the relationships of adolescence probably provide an interlude during which the relationship to parents can become modified to suit the new conditions, and at the same time a new type of relationship to a potential spouse can be developed. Although peer relationships continue to be important, they never carry the same intensity of emotion that is carried by family relationships. For example, bereavement responses to the loss of a peer are very rarely as emotionally disturbing as to loss of a parent, spouse or child. Robert Weiss's studies [Weiss, 1975] in this area are the best I know of. As you say, I think there can be no doubt that stable marital relationships are of survival value. I suspect that in almost every culture the children of single parents are at a greater risk of coming to harm than are the children of two parents. Children undoubtedly have a considerable stake in keeping their parents together.

On the 12th May, I sent Bowlby two papers of mine (Bacciagaluppi, 1985a,b).

I regret that quantitative research is so far removed from in-depth knowledge of individual cases. For instance, my wife's recurrence became clinically evident and led to last year's operation in June, after her mother had died in April. Quantitative research can, at best, confirm such correlations, but knowledge of the relationship can lead to much more detailed connections. I obviously have a strong personal motivation to pursue this subject, but I agree that these ideas still need to be elaborated.

On the 7th October 1984, I mentioned the Milan seminar and regretted that I had already taken on another engagement. In his reply of the 22nd October, Bowlby wrote,

I am most distressed to hear that you will be away from Milan when I visit there in April, since I had been looking forward to meeting you then. But should you be in London next summer between mid-June and the end of July we shall be able to meet here.

He then commented on the two papers I had sent him.

I have now read them with much interest and am glad to know they have been accepted for publication. The one linking attachment theory to Fromm's ideas [Bacciagaluppi, 1985b] I found especially illuminating, as it is a link I was unaware of. Since Fromm is influenced by Marxist ideas, it comes as a surprise to me that he gives so much weight to biological factors. So many East European communists seem to think human nature is infinitely malleable. I am, of course, delighted by the extent to which you find attachment theory useful. Such few comments as I have are mainly only terminological, although I believe unsuitable terminology frequently obscures the truth and gives rise to misunderstanding. I believe it is a mistake to refer to a parent who is subject to anxious attachment and who makes demands on his or her child as being 'infantile'. In English it is a very disparaging adjective, though I believe it may not be so in Italian. Ordinary healthy adults seek care from others when in distress. In the cases you are discussing, the fact that care is sought is in no way pathological. What is pathological is that it is directed towards a child instead of another adult, owing to adverse experiences in the parents' earlier life. For the same reason I think it mistaken to refer to an adult's 'dependency needs' as being in any way 'residual'. In addition, I'm afraid I continue to regard the use of 'symbiosis' as unfortunate. In biology a symbiotic relationship is a relationship between two organisms (of different species), who each contribute to the other's survival. The relationship is therefore symmetrical. In the case of the healthy mother–child relationship, it is not symmetrical, since the child does not contribute to the mother's survival – indeed he enters the balance sheet at a cost. The opposite is true where the relationship is inverted. In neither case therefore is it symmetrical, being heavily weighted one way in the healthy case and the other in the unhealthy one. It is this asymmetry that the term 'symbiosis' obscures.

To this I replied on the 11th November:

In addition to that opportunity of meeting, I wonder if you will also be in Zürich next August. The International Federation of Psychoanalysis [actually, the International Federation of Psychoanalytic Societies, IFPS] (co-founded by Fromm some years ago [to be precise, in 1962] as an alternative to the IPA) organizes the VII International Forum of Psychoanalysis in Zürich on August 14–18. The theme is 'The Meaning of Psychoanalysis in Our Time'. . . . At that meeting, I intend to present a paper on 'Attachment theory as an alternative basis of psychoanalysis'. . . . My presentation could be a synthesis of the papers written so far. Basically, I suggest that a renewal of psychoanalysis may be accomplished by retaining the psychoanalytic method (use of free associations and dreams, analysis of transference, etc.) and adopting attachment theory as an alternative theoretical framework. . . . If retrospective, in-depth studies of individual cases, carried out according to your alternative viewpoint, yield fresh insights which lend themselves to verification through prospective studies, they may in turn make a contribution to the theory. I am very grateful for your comments on the papers. I meant to use the term 'infantile' in a merely

descriptive sense, but even then I realize that it may prove inappropriate if it conveys the idea that adults do not have attachment needs.
On the other hand, it is true that in the inverted relationship the
parent's adverse experiences took place in childhood. It should be
possible to convey the idea that, in these cases, unsatisfied childhood
needs are carried over into adult life, leading to an exaggeration or a
distortion of attachment behaviour, as compared to the normal adult
situation. I also appreciated your comments on the term 'symbiosis',
which stimulated me to do some more thinking on the matter. Both
my University biology textbook and Webster's dictionary consider
'symbiosis' the more general term (the living together of two dissimi-
lar organisms), which includes three categories: parasitism (the relationship is advantageous for one organism, harmful for the other),
mutualism (advantageous for both), and commensalism (advantageous for one, indifferent for the other). However, I have been using
the term not as defined in biology but as already used by psychoanalytic writers such as Margaret Mahler and Harold Searles [1965].
The situation referred to has been described by many other psychoanalytic authors as 'lack of differentation between self and object'. At
a family level, Searles [1965] and Slipp [1973] speak of 'family symbiosis', Minuchin [1974] of 'blurred boundaries', and Bowen [1978] of
'undifferentiated families'. To avoid an inappropriate use of the term
'symbiosis', maybe such situations could be better described by the
term 'undifferentation'. The assessors of my British paper also objected to 'symbiosis', so I omitted it entirely from the definitive version.
. . . Undifferentation seems to be one characteristic of inverted relationships, where the child's differentation and autonomy, leading to
separation, is threatening to the parent. Another characteristic of
mother–child relationships, as you point out, is that of asymmetry. In
the case of the inverted relationship, I wonder if another biological
term would fit, namely 'parasitism'. . . . Concerning Fromm, he was in
no way connected with East European communism. He considered it
'pseudo-Marxism'. Instead, he was an admirer of Marx's youthful
philosophical works, such as the *Economic and Philosophic Manuscripts
of 1844*, which he discussed in *Marx's Concept of Man* [Fromm, 1961]. I
tried to convey this difference by using the adjective 'Marxian' in my
manuscript. The American editor must have been unaware of this
difference, and changed the adjective to 'Marxist' in the edited
version. I did not argue, in order not to put obstacles in the way of
publication, but maybe I should have followed your example and
stood firm on the matter of terminology. Fromm's earlier works,
which I quote in my paper, do not refer explicitly to biology, but are

grounded in the tradition of Western philosophy. It is I who call attention to the affinity between Fromm's ideas and the ethological viewpoint. Later, Fromm made explicit reference to ethology in *The Anatomy of Human Destructiveness* [Fromm, 1973].

I wrote again on the 21st January 1985.

First of all, I wish to thank you for the reprint of your paper on 'Violence in the Family'. . . . I greatly appreciated the extension of your enquiries to this other category of real-life events, and entirely agree with your evaluation of Freud's dismissal of the seduction theory (p. 9). [Bowlby (1988b, p. 78) speaks of Freud's "disastrous volte-face in 1897"]. You have probably heard of *The Assault on Truth*, a book by Jeff Masson which discusses this matter. This book has just been translated into Italian, and I was recently one of the discussants at a meeting with Dr. Masson in Milan. Maybe Masson is to be criticized for publishing unauthorized material, but the Freudians could equally be criticized for omitting important passages from Freud's published correspondence. Later, an article attacking Masson appeared on the *Academy Forum*. I disagreed with it and submitted a Letter to the Editor to express my alternative views [Bacciagaluppi, 1985c]. I am also pleased to inform you that my abstract on 'Attachment theory as an alternative basis of psychoanalysis' has been accepted at the Zürich meeting. It is an ambitious subject, and I shall have to do a lot more work on it. It is an attempt to carry out your suggestion of using attachment theory 'to construct a new metapsychology' (p. 12 of your paper).

Bowlby replied on the 13th February 1985.

This is to thank you for your two letters . . . and to apologize for not answering earlier. . . . I am glad to know your paper on attachment theory has been accepted for presentation. . . . It will be most interesting to hear how it is received. I shall not be going myself. But I am looking forward to your visit to London during the latter half of July when I hope we can meet.

He then told me about the recent book by Greenberg and Mitchell, *Object Relations in Psychoanalytic Theory* (Greenberg & Mitchell, 1983).

It is a lucid presentation and discussion. There is not a lot about attachment theory, but what there is is accurate and sympathetic. Nevertheless, they fail, I think, to give any attention to the crucial point about real-life experiences, and I feel sure this is the biggest issue confronting psychoanalysis today. I am much in agreement with your letter to the Editor of *Academy Forum*. There has been a concerted attempt to denigrate Masson's book, which I found interesting. It has one rather serious weakness, however, namely a complete absence of any evidence supporting his view that real-life events are crucial. He should at least have referred to some of the work now published, especially the findings on father–daughter incest which have been appearing. Without his referring to the evidence it is easy for critics to dismiss him, which is a great pity.

Actually, in the Preface to the Penguin Edition of his book, Masson concurred with Bowlby:

> Many women, sympathetic to the research I have done in this book, have been puzzled by my lack of explicit recognition of the work done by feminist authors in the field of sexual abuse of children. . . . I believe, in retrospect, that this was a mistake. . . . It now strikes me as wrong not to acknowledge my predecessors in this field.

He then goes on to quote the literature, and, specifically, Judith Herman's book on father–daughter incest (Herman, 1981), which is possibly what Bowlby had in mind.

In my reply of the 1st April, 1985, I said,

> The book by Greenberg and Mitchell is indeed very valuable as an up-to-date overview of psychoanalytic theories. I have two objections to the section on attachment theory. (1) On p. 186 they say that 'because of these efforts to place psychoanalytic data within an extrapsychoanalytic framework', your theory 'cannot stand as a distinctly and purely psychoanalytic model per se'. Here they seem to have missed the point entirely and fallen into the hermeneutic fallacy. To have used the framework of modern biology is precisely your merit. Otherwise, psychoanalysis lends itself to the attacks of the philosophers of science. Popper had already delivered one [Popper, 1963]. The latest is: Adolf Grünbaum, *The Foundations of Psychoanalysis. A Philosophical critique* [Grünbaum, 1984]. (2) The authors claim that you underestimate the mother's emotional absence. But you explicitly state the equivalence of physical absence and emotional unavailability on p. 23 of your second volume, and Chapter 14 is entirely devoted to this subject. Maybe their impression is an artifact due to the fact that most of the empirical work you report concerns physical absence, due either

to separation or loss, possibly because these clear-cut events lend themselves more readily to quantitative study. Dr. Bemporad wrote to me recently saying that he too feels the need for an ethological base on which to ground psychoanalytic theory. . . . Within the last two years, a meeting on attachment and one on separation have been organized within the interpersonal–cultural area. These all seem to be signs that the time is ripe to try and unify the field of psychoanalysis with your new paradigm. So far, the existence of many competing schools seems to indicate that the field is in a pre-paradigm phase, as Kuhn [1962] would say.

Shortly before the seminar, on the 13th April 1985, Bowlby sent me a handwritten note saying that he and his wife would spend two weeks at the Castelli di Gargonza (a medieval town near Arezzo). Thus, he combined the seminar with a trip to Tuscany.

On the 20th May, I wrote,

Just now I am engaged in reading *Cognitive Processes and Emotional Disorders* by Guidano and Liotti [1983], with which I suppose you are familiar, for it is dedicated to you [Bowlby had met them in Rome, as he states in the introduction to "On knowing what you are not supposed to know and feeling what you are not supposed to feel", which is Lecture 6 of *A Secure Base* (Bowlby, 1988b, p. 99), where he writes: "I was surprised and delighted to find how much we had in common. One consequence of our meeting was an invitation to contribute to a volume on *Cognition and Psychotherapy* being edited by Michael Mahoney and Arthur Freeman [1985]. This provided an opportunity to expand the original brief paper and led to the version that follows."] I find it an important work, which integrates attachment theory not with psychoanalysis but with behaviour and cognitive therapy. The authors avowedly leave psychoanalysis, both Freudian and neo-Freudian, out of consideration. They thus give the impression of a rather skewed selection of the literature. For instance, they quote Popper's concept of the 'looking-glass effect', but fail to mention Lacan's and Winnicott's discussions of the mirror function and Sullivan's concept of 'reflected appraisals' [which Bowlby, instead, discusses in the footnote on p. 234 of *Loss*].

After the seminar, on the 22nd July, I at last met Bowlby at the Tavistock to discuss my paper on "Attachment theory as an alternative basis of psychoanalysis". He had prepared some written remarks, and added others verbally. This is one of the written remarks:

As far as attachment behaviour is concerned there is less of a discrepancy between biological and cultural evolution than you suggest. Although predators are no longer a risk in western cultures, there are many new dangers, e.g. motorcars, household equipment etc. There is good evidence that the principal victims are children who are not in the company of an adult. Thus attachment behaviour continues to have survival value.

Here are some of his verbal remarks, from my notes:

domestication as model: Bowlby tends to accept the possibility that innate behavioural tendencies in the child can be exploited (his term); symbiosis: he gave the example of a parent who, on account of his/her own needs, says to a child: 'We (feel one way or another)'; Bowlby suggests calling this 'identity confusion'; Bemporad's [Jules Bemporad, later Professor of Clinical Psychiatry at New York Medical College] idea of an early discrepancy between two different modes of communication (verbal and non-verbal): Bowlby agrees with me that the discrepancy would originally have been only potential.

After incorporating Bowlby's remarks into the text, I presented it in August in Zürich, at the VII International Forum of Psychoanalysis. It was later published in an American journal (Bacciagaluppi, 1989a), after having been rejected by two other journals. As I said to Bowlby in a letter of the 24th August 1986, "explicit suggestions of a major paradigm shift are hard to accept".

After the Zürich meeting, I wrote three letters reporting on the meeting. In the first, of the 27th August, I wrote,

I wish to thank you once more for having given me so much of your time last month in London. The conversation with you, your comments on my paper and your own papers provided me with a psychological and theoretical 'safe base' which helped me face the Zürich meeting with greater assurance. At the meeting, the major components were the Americans and the German-speaking group. Among the Americans were many neo-Freudians. There were also numerous participants from Latin America (several Brazilians were Lacanian) and Scandinavian countries. There was nobody from Britain or France. I was the only Italian. . . . A student of psychology at Zürich said she would show my paper to one of her teachers, Prof. Bischof, who is very interested in attachment theory. . . . Other people were interested in my work because of its references to Fromm. They were Jorge Silva-Garcia, a Mexican pupil of Fromm's, and Rainer Funk, from Germany, Fromm's literary executor. . . . He said that Fromm had bought *Attachment* and annotated it. . . . Among the other contributions I heard, I found one observation of particular interest. Dr. Shatan, of New York, discussing the impact of collective disasters on children, remarked that children involved in natural disasters do better than victims of man-made disasters, presumably because natural disasters don't create a sense of rupture of human trust [this is Chaim Shatan, who, together with Robert Jay Lifton, gave support to traumatised Vietnam veterans; the principle he presented in Zürich had been incorporated in the definition of trauma in *DSM-III* [American Psychiatric Association, 1980]]. To conclude, I hope I have made some contribution to a wider dissemination of your ideas in clinical circles.

In my second letter I spoke of Dr Videgård, a Swedish psychologist who was in the same panel as I.

He spoke on a rather circumscribed subject: an outcome study of primal therapy (Janov's 'primal scream' therapy). He later sent me a monograph of his on this matter (Videgård, 1983). In the theoretical part of his book he shows complete convergence with me concerning the importance of your work. Like Greenberg and Mitchell, he divides psychoanalytic teories in two groups, which he calls 'drive-oriented' and 'trauma-relations oriented'. He too is convinced that psychoanalysis needs a new paradigm and believes that your theory can provide it. He diverges from me in trying to integrate your theory with Kohut's Self-psychology. This reminded me of my own earlier attempt to integrate your theory with Margaret Mahler's. I told him that you had pointed out the incompatibility of the two positions.

In the third letter, of the 13th September, I say,

I received some more feedback on Zürich from Norbert Bischof, who worked with Konrad Lorenz at Seewiesen and then at the California Institute of Technology, and is now Professor of Psychology at Zürich University. He is very interested in attachment theory and sent me two papers of his in English. In June, a book of his appeared in German: *Das Rätsel Ödipus* (The Oedipus Riddle) [Bischof, 1985] [in this book, the author repeatedly quotes Bowlby].

Bowlby replied on the 8th January 1986,

I am very glad your paper was well received in Zürich and that you have made some useful contacts. Norbert Bischof I know a little and have often referred to his 1975 paper on a systems approach [Bischof, 1975]. I had not known of his book, however, and only wish I were able to read German. He is a valuable person. Dr. Videgård is a new name to me and I am glad to know of him. I will mention him to another of my psychotherapeutic friends in Stockholm, Mrs. Emmy Gut, who has a good grasp of attachment theory. She has published a couple of papers on depression . . . and is now working on a book [this is *Productive and Unproductive Depression*, which will be published in 1989 with a foreword by Bowlby]. During October I was in Denver, Colorado and then a week at the Menninger, where there are three qualified analysts who are well-informed and enthusiastic about attachment theory. I gave several lectures and took part in case conferences. As usual it turned out that it is clinicians seeing adult patients who have most to learn. Those in child and family psychiatry are much better informed. Since returning I have been busy drafting a long paper on the psychotherapeutic implications of attachment theory [this is possibly 'Attachment, communication and the therapeutic process', which will appear as Lecture 8 of *A Secure Base* as an amplification of an earlier paper], which I shall be using during another lecturing visit to North America, planned for next May, mainly Washington, D.C., where I am to give the Adolf Meyer Lecture to the American Psychiatric Association, and then Toronto. Next academic year I am determined to stay at home in order to finish my study of Charles Darwin [this led to Bowlby's last book, which appeared in 1990 and in which, out of gratitude for the powerful theoretical framework provided by Darwin, Bowlby expresses parental concern for Darwin's ill health].

In a PS he adds, "I was very glad to see your paper on Inversion of Parent–Child Relationships in the recent number of the British Journal of Medical Psychology [this is Bacciagaluppi, 1985a]".

On the 18th February 1986, I wrote,

While doing some research on the role of aggression in attachment theory, I found a reference in Fromm's *Anatomy of Human Destructiveness* [Fromm, 1973] to a book you co-authored in 1939 on *Personal Aggressiveness and War* [Durbin & Bowlby, 1939], of which I know nothing. I would be very grateful if you could tell me if the book is still available, or if a summary of it exists; also, what your present position is regarding the subject of the book.

On the 2nd March 1986, Bowlby wrote saying he had sent me the pre-war book he had written together with his friend Evan Durbin [in it he wrote a dedication to me]. "I have plenty of spare copies and I am glad to find a good home for one!" In his letter, which is written by hand and not typewritten as usual, he says,

> Without reading it through carefully, I am reluctant to guess what my present attitude to our theses would be. No doubt I should use a more sociobiological perspective now than I did then. My friend Evan Durbin, alas, lost his life in an accident in 1948. He was always eager to apply psychoanalytic insights to social and political questions. I was more cautious.

In this letter, Bowlby started addressing me as "Dear Marco", but I was too much in awe to reciprocate, and in my replies stuck to "Dear Dr Bowlby" to the end.

I replied on the 27th March:

> I did not reply sooner because I wanted to read the book first. Now I have nearly finished it and feel I can make some comments on it. I like this book very much. I find it is a valuable contribution to the study of an issue which is, unfortunately, still very relevant. Methodologically, some things may be dated. Today, I am sure, you would quote observations on animals in the wild rather than Zuckermann's observations on animals in captivity [this is Solly Zuckerman [1932], the British government's scientific consultant; in Bowlby's pre-war book his name is spelled with a double 'n', in German fashion, but actually it should be spelt with only one 'n'; many years later, Zuckerman [1982] turned his attention to the armament spiral between the USA and the Soviet Union]. On the other hand, in this book you make use of the observation of children, a very important source of data which Fromm neglected in his own much later work on aggressiveness. As regards content, there are many things with which I find myself entirely in agreement. First of all, the description of the two-phase vicissitudes of aggression on pp. 16–18 (frustration leads to simple aggression, the punishment of simple aggression leads to transformed aggression), and the corresponding remedies suggested on p. 41. Another point is the emphasis on peaceful cooperation as a characteristic of man (although, to be sure, limited to the group to which one belongs). This is the reason for which Fromm quoted your book. In particular (p. 6), care for the good of

others is viewed as one component of cooperative behaviour. This is very relevant to the current interest in altruistic, or prosocial, behaviour. It is a pity you interrupted this line of research, although, methodologically, its use of animal and children data may be regarded as a precursor of your later work. I suppose the interruption was due to the war and, later, to the death of your co-author and the fact that you devoted yourself to building up attachment theory. I think it would be worth while to remind the public of your book and to try and integrate it with later work on the same subject, and I would like to make some contribution in this direction. For this end I wish to put a question to you. You signed only the second part of the book, but I am wondering if there are not contributions of yours also in the first part, in particular, the discussion on aggression on pp. 16–18 which I mentioned above.

## Bowlby answered on the 21st April:

I am glad you found our book . . . of interest. It was written in 1937. Although Evan Durbin and I were each responsible for the drafting of the parts we signed, the ideas had been shared in discussions over the previous eight years, during much of which we had lived in the same house. Evan was a remarkable person and a great loss. The son of a Baptist minister, he won scholarships to Oxford. His first degree was in zoology, but his lasting interest was in politics – democratic socialism. Instead of going on in biology, therefore, he spent another two years at Oxford reading Philosophy, Politics and Economics in which he took first-class honours. He then became a lecturer in economics at the London School of Economics and also played a major part in Labour politics, standing (unsuccessfully) for Parliament. At Oxford he was a friend of my older brother. Evan and I arrived in London together in September 1929 when I started my clinical training at University College Hospital. We shared a flat for the next three years, until he got married. Two years later he, and his wife and baby, and I decided to acquire a house and to divide it into two apartments. So you see we saw a lot of each other. I had started training in psychoanalysis when I started at Medical School and Evan was deeply interested in it. His concern was largely political: how can a better understanding of human nature contribute to the political goals he had set himself? I taught him all the psychoanalysis he knew. He used to pick my brains, but before he accepted anything he would challenge me for the evidence. This was good for both of us. So the ideas in the book were shared, but we were writing for different readerships. Of course, we each commented on and revised each other's drafts. The book was his initiative when we realized war was imminent, and he pulled me in. I really felt psychoanalytic understanding was in too much of a muddle for it to be ready to be applied to social problems, and that the venture was premature. So my concern was with the long-term problem of developing psychoanalysis as a scientific discipline, which I knew would be a long-term endeavour. As a politician, Evan was concerned to get practical results as soon as possible. Soon after the book was published we were both engaged in war work, but after he was elected to Parliament in 1945 he was still eager to pursue the social and political implications of psychoanalysis. I continued to feel it was premature, but of course we remained close friends until his untimely death in 1948. I am naturally very glad you are thinking of doing some further work in this area and will look forward to the results.

Bowlby wrote again on the 31st July, but the letter is not in my records. I wrote on the 24th August,

I am devoting this holiday to drafting an article on your pre-war book. Your letter of the 21st April confirms that, in addition to the part signed by you, the psychological ideas of the first part can also be ascribed to you. I think this may justify my considering them as precursors of later ideas of yours. I put off this work until the holidays partly because of my busy practice, but maybe also because of a certain discouragement, due to the fact that my Zürich paper has been rejected by two leading neo-Freudian journals, *Contemporary Psychoanalysis* and the *Journal of the American Academy of Psychoanalysis*. This paper may have objective faults. It is a preliminary suggestion and not a thoroughly elaborated piece of work. Still, these objections could have led to a request for revision and not to an outright rejection. Maybe, explicit suggestions of a major paradigm shift are hard to accept.

On the 4th September, Bowlby sent a handwritten note.

At present, I'm on holiday in the Isle of Skye and have been taking a good deal of exercise, tho' otherwise idle. Your holiday task sounds amusing and I'll be interested to see your article. I seem to be becoming an historical monument! A TV company is making some programs [the American spelling is in the original] about my work, to be shown on my 80th birthday next February.

On the 1st October 1986, Bowlby commented on a draft I had sent on the 8th September of a paper on the pre-war book:

I have been reading your article with much interest, and with admira-
tion for the clarity and accuracy of your exposition. It also makes me
quite proud of this early work! . . . Only a couple of points for possible additions occur to me: 1. I probably failed to tell you that, before
he became an economist, Durbin had taken an honours degree in
Zoology at Oxford and had made a special study of evolution theory.
This common background in biology was a crucial element in the ability of an economist and a psychoanalyst to collaborate. (Reading your
article has drawn my attention to the extent to which I was ethologi-
cally oriented before I had ever heard of ethology, and also of the
extent to which Evan Durbin and I shared an evolutionary point of
view.) 2. Although we give attention to the tendency for physical
punishment of children by parents to provoke aggressive behaviour in
the children, I think we give too little attention to the long-term effects
of the strong tendency of children to model themselves on (or identify
with) the behaviour of parents. Furthermore, we omit altogether the
extremely adverse effects on children of being physically battered by
disturbed parents; such children can become horribly aggressive to all
and sundry.

On the 6th January 1987, I informed Bowlby that my paper on his
pre-war book had been rejected by one British journal. I also sent my
very best wishes for his eightieth birthday in February.

In his reply of the 11th February, he advised me to send my paper
to *Free Associations*, which had just published a long interview with
him (Bowlby, Figlio, & Young, 1986). This journal eventually accepted
my paper (Bacciagaluppi, 1989b).

On the 1st July 1987, I wrote,

The other day, at a very short notice indeed, I received an invitation
from Prof. Molnar to take part in a symposium in Hungary in August.
He had already written to me last year saying he was very interested in
attachment theory. He told me he hopes you will chair this meeting.

On the 8th July, Bowlby wrote,

I am delighted to know that you are able to accept Professor Molnar's
invitation and will be interested to hear how you find the state of
opinion about our areas of work in Hungary. Unfortunately I cannot
be there myself – too many things to do. We have just ended a big
conference on attachment theory over here with a number of my
American friends giving papers. It was a great success and generated
much interest and enthusiasm.

HAMPSTEAD HEALTH AUTHORITY

# The Tavistock Clinic
### CHILD AND FAMILY DEPARTMENT

TAVISTOCK CENTRE, 120 BELSIZE LANE, LONDON, NW3 5BA

Telephone: 01-435 7111 Ext.

JB/DES                                              11th February 1987

Dr. Marco Bacciagaluppi
Via Adolo 46
Milano 20125
ITALY

Dear Marco,

     Just a line to express sympathy on the third
rejection of your paper and gratitude to you for your
good wishes for my 80th - at the end of the month.  I
am glad you are drafting another paper and hope that it
meets with a better fate.

     There is a new journal, FREE ASSOCIATIONS, that
might well be interested to publish your original paper,
and I am enclosing particulars of it.  The recent number
contains a long interview the editors did with me.
They are probably more interested in the history of our
field than editors of other journals.

With all good wishes

Yours

John Bowlby, M.D.

Bowlby's letter to Marco Bacciagaluppi of 11 February 1987.

I replied on the 17th July:

One thing I am curious to find out is whether Prof. Molnar's interest
in attachment theory has been influenced, directly or indirectly, by the
Hungarian school of psychoanalysis, which you discuss in the Appendix to *Attachment*, and also whether any members of this school are
still alive.

On the 14th September 1987, I reported on the meeting I attended
in Hungary (Bacciagaluppi, 1987b).

The level of some of the Hungarian contributions was high, especially that of Eva Banyai. . . . Privately, much dissatisfaction was expressed [with the still prevailing Communist regime]. . . . Apart from my own contribution [Bacciagaluppi, 1987a], there were no direct references to your work, but several contributions were related to it, especially that of Wulf Schiefenhövel on cultural expressions of grief. Schiefenhövel is a collaborator of Eibl-Eibesfeldt at Seewiesen – the institute which used to be directed by Lorenz. . . . As regards the influence of psychoanalysis, the Hungarian participants were all academics, and no official reference to psychoanalysis was made. In private conversations, however, several Hungarians admitted having contacts (including training) with the surviving Hungarian analytic circles. [Bowlby discusses the Hungarian school of psychoanalysis in the Appendix to *Attachment* [Bowlby, 1969]].

Bowlby replied on the 24th September:

In your account [Bacciagaluppi. 1987b] I think there is a rather serious omission. . . . In describing the influence of Sandor Ferenczi and the Hungarian School you should, I think, mention Michael Balint who had almost as much influence in promoting the British Object Relations School as did Melanie Klein.

On the 16th December 1987, Bowlby wrote about the IFPS meeing to be held in Rio in October 1989.

I do not anticipate being in Rio then but would like to call your attention to some workers there who are great enthusiasts for attachment theory. They have founded a school of psychoanalysis and ethology and have also started a journal in which a number of my papers have been translated into Portuguese.

He then gives me the address of Dr Elizabeth Brazil Paulon, the Director of the School.
On the 22nd December 1987, I submitted a research idea.

A colleague of mine . . . and I are connected with an Italian group concerned with the dangers of the nuclear age. We plan to apply for a grant to the MacArthur Foundation of Chicago to support some research on the subject. Here is a brief outline of the theory behind the project. In facing the dangers of the nuclear age, it is important to define the psychological resources which can be mobilized and the

obstacles to their mobilization. According to a non-Lorenzian ethological theory of aggressiveness, which can be based on your own work,
as well as on that of Fromm [1973] and Scott [1958], defensive aggressiveness is an innate resource to any danger threatening the organism.
The prospect of a nuclear accident or a nuclear war is an extreme
example of a danger to the organism which should elicit defensive
aggressiveness. It is suggested that one structural obstacle to this
mobilization is the peasant culture, which is a patriarchal, authoritarian cultural development superimposed onto our innate tendencies.
The transition from the peasant culture to modern society, whilst
giving rise to short-term maladjustment, may lead to a solution of the
long-term maladjustment due to the earlier transition from the
hunter–gatherer to the peasant culture. The breakdown of the peasant
culture may liberate innate behavioural tendencies such as defensive
aggressiveness. Whilst certain technological and economic developments in modern society cause increased danger to our survival, other
developments may mobilize the response against this danger. This
hypothesis could be tested by comparing the responses to the nuclear
threat of schoolchildren of urban and rural areas in Italy. These data
could be related to socioeconomic variables and integrated with pro-
jective tests and depth inquiries, following the model of the Mexican
study of Fromm and Maccoby [1970]. To allow for the short-term
maladjustment due to urbanization, the number of generations since
urbanization took place should be taken into account.

I then ask if he would accept to be one of our professional references
and if I could also quote him as one of the persons to visit on a study
tour.

Bowlby replied on the 7th January 1988:

I'm afraid I am not hopeful. The project seems to me exceedingly difficult to do in a way that would satisfy a foundation like the MacArthur,
who use rather strict criteria in judging proposals. . . . On the other
hand, by all means name me as one the persons you would plan to
visit on your study tour.

On the 11th July 1988, I said, "My colleague and I appreciated your
caution. It led us to reconsider the whole idea more carefully". I then
spoke of my third attempt to have my Zürich manuscript published,
and on the 5th August I wrote, "After three years, and at the third
attempt, my Zürich paper . . . has at last been accepted by the *American*

*Journal of Psychoanalysis.* I hope this publication will contribute to the clinical application of your theory".

On the 21st September, Bowlby wrote, "I was delighted to hear from you last month that your Zurich paper has found a haven with the *American Journal of Psychoanalysis.* I think this will in fact be an excellent place for its publication [this is where Bowlby had published "Violence in the family" in 1984]".

Here is our last exchange. On the 24th November 1988, I wrote,

> I have been invited to contribute a chapter to an American book on the narcissistic personality [Bacciagaluppi, 1993]. This is an opportunity to apply your framework to a specific clinical problem. I would be glad of any suggestions. You do not seem to have addressed this problem in particular. There is an obvious pathway leading from the avoidant attachment pattern to the lack of empathy of the narcissistic personality (as described, e.g., by Kernberg [1975]). What needs to be clarified is the origin of another ingredient, the compensatory inflated self-concept.

On the 4th January 1989, Bowlby replied,

> I am delighted to hear that you have found a 'good home' for your paper on "The role of aggressiveness in the work of John Bowlby". . . . I am glad to hear that you will be writing a chapter on the narcissistic personality, and agree with you completely that it is an outcome of a strongly avoidant attachment pattern. The high self-esteem such people claim is, as you say, a compensatory fabrication which, when called seriously in question, collapses and gives way to depression. A great many avoidantly attached children grow up to have some variant of this personality, I suspect. We do not know in detail the kind of childhood relationships that give rise to it. My guess would a fairly stable relationship with a mother who gives the child fully adequate material care but is emotionally cold and rejecting.

I wrote again on the 19th March 1990, but received no reply. On the 11th October, I received a note from his secretary, Dorothy Southern, announcing a Memorial Service for Bowlby, who had died on the 2nd September. I replied expressing my sympathy to her.

> You worked with him for many years, and his death must be a great loss for you. It is also a loss for me. I considered Dr. Bowlby a great teacher, and he was always ready to give his opinion and his advice.

My friend Jules Bemporad commented, "He was the last of the giants in our field."

## The seminar

I succeeded in transmitting my enthusiasm for Bowlby to numerous colleagues, who were then very active in organising the seminar in Milan, with the title "Research and psychotherapy", on the 27th and 28th April 1985. The year before, Emilia Fumagalli ("Milly" for short) had gone for training at the Tavistock. She suggested the seminar to Bowlby, who accepted, much to her surprise, for it was more than she had hoped for. Germana Agnetti and Angelo Barbato gave hospitality to Bowlby and his wife, and Germana's mother to the whole seminar. The night before the seminar, Bowlby gave a lecture in the University, on which I do not have further information. At the seminar, Ferruccio Osimo did a splendid job chairing and translating from one language to the other. He later translated Bowlby's theoretical introduction and published it in an Italian journal (Bowlby, 1986). His wife, Claudia Ferrandes, saw to the audio recording. Leopolda Pelizzaro, Ferruccio himself, and Milly each presented a case, which was then discussed by Bowlby. Ferruccio kept the audiotapes of the seminar all these years. At the beginning of 2011, I thought of publishing the seminar, so Ferruccio brought me the tapes and I transcribed them. I shall ask these colleagues to add their own comments to mine. In particular, Milly presents her case once more. She did so at the seminar, but the corresponding part is missing from the tape, which contains only Bowlby's comments on the case. In the text, John Bowlby, Emilia Fumagalli, Ferruccio Osimo, and Leopolda Pelizzaro are designated by their initials (JB, EF, FO, and LP). The other participants are kept anonymous. JB, EF, and FO spoke directly into the microphone, whereas the other participants spoke from the floor, and at times are scarcely audible. Some of the participants spoke directly in English, the other comments were translated by Ferruccio. Some of these comments are reported verbatim. When I summarise them, I use square brackets. Aside from the theoretical introduction, every word uttered by Bowlby is included.

Germana Agnetti and Angelo Barbato, who gave hospitality to Bowlby and his wife at their home, have added their own account of the seminar to this book. I have translated their contribution, as well as those of Emilia Fumagalli, Leopolda Pelizzaro, and Claudia Ferrandes, into English. Ferruccio Osimo wrote his two contributions directly in English.

There were around thirty participants, all psychiatrists, psychologists, and psychotherapists. Many had a traditional psychoanalytic, or a Kleinian, background, due to the influence of the Italian Kleinian, Franco Fornari

At the beginning of the seminar there is a theoretical introduction on "Defensive processes in the light of attachment theory", in which Bowlby presents views published elsewhere. He replaces Freud's energy model and the notion of "dammed-up libido" with control theory, which explains the child's attachment behaviour in normal circumstances as a system set to maintain the child's proximity to its mother because of its survival value. In pathological circumstances, following certain sorts of separation, the deactivation of this system leads to the child's detached attitude. More specifically, at an unconscious level there is a defensive selective exclusion of information inflow. As an example of emotional detachment and compulsive self-sufficiency, Bowlby presents Mrs G, a case which he had already discussed in *Loss* (Bowlby, 1980, p. 368) and will take up again in *A Secure Base* (Bowlby, 1988b, p. 68). The patient's childhood was characterised by severe relational traumas. He regards her condition as due to the deactivation of the attachment behavioural system. Following the recent work of the cognitive psychologists, he describes this deactivation as due to the selective exclusion of incoming signals that would activate attachment behaviour. This is what Freud called repression. He says that her condition could be described as schizoid (Fairbairn, 1940), or as false self (Winnicott, 1960), or as narcissistic (Kohut, 1971). Therapy "restored this patient's feeling life". Specifically, she became able to experience "her analyst's genuine concern to help her" in the present, and the memory of painful events in the past. Bowlby then mentions a case of his own, of a woman who tried to irritate him. "What she was afraid of, it seemed clear, was becoming attached to me, because, in her experience, to become attached to somebody could lead only to rejection."

At this point, Bowlby mentions the usefulness of Freud's clinical theorising, in contrast with his metapsychology. He then goes on to point out that the selective exclusion of thoughts and feelings is often due to the active intervention of parents. Children often exclude information, concerning either external events (typically, one parent's suicide) or their own feelings, "to conform to their parents' wishes". He also mentions situations of a more subtle sort that require defensive exclusion, such as the inversion of the normal parent–child relationship or a parent's own traumatic childhood. This was the subject of an earlier paper (Bowlby, 1979), which will be reprinted in *A Secure Base* (Bowlby, 1988b, p. 99).

Other authors cited by Bowlby in his theoretical introduction are Cain and Fast (1972) and Alice Miller (1979). This is Alice Miller's first book, *The Drama of the Gifted Child*. Bowlby quotes twice from this book. He obviously detected in her a kindred author. All Miller's later books are characterised by deep concern for childhood trauma.

I believe the clinical part of the seminar is of special interest. Bowlby presents clinical material throughout his published works, but, to my knowledge, the only paper specifically devoted to therapy is Lecture 8 in *A Secure Base*, titled "Attachment, communication, and the therapeutic process" (Bowlby, 1988b, p. 137), to which I shall return in the "Concluding remarks" section.

Right at the beginning, one participant speaks of "constructions". Bowlby replies, "My emphasis is more on the patient discovering than me giving reconstructions." He then adds, "the more we know about the traumatic events of childhood . . . the more we are able to be useful companions in exploration." Here, Bowlby reveals a new emphasis in his work. In contrast with Melanie Klein, who supervised him, his concern had always been with "real-life events", among which he emphasised separation, but, shortly before the seminar, in 1983, he gave in America a paper on "Violence in the family", which was published in an American journal the next year (Bowlby, 1984) and which will be later reprinted in *A Secure Base* (Bowlby, 1988b, p. 77). In this paper, he says, "As psychoanalysts and psychotherapists we have been appallingly slow to wake up to the prevalence and far-reaching consequences of violent behaviour between members of a family", and he then speaks of Freud's "famous, and in my view *disastrous, volte-face* in 1897" (my emphasis), when Freud denied the reality of sexual abuse. Here, Bowlby explicitly joins the vast trauma literature that, after Ferenczi's pioneering efforts in the last years of his life (Ferenczi, 1933), had been growing up in those years and had led shortly before the seminar to the incorporation of PTSD (post traumatic stress disorder) into the *DSM-III* in 1980. Bowlby expressed his appreciation of Ferenczi in the Foreword to Ian Suttie's pre-war book (Bowlby, 1988a).

Some circumscribed topics arise: the difference between dependence and attachment; drug addiction; autism; the difference between representational model and internal object; the various patterns of attachment; the number of sessions per week. One participant actually thinks that Bowlby's concepts are similar to Melanie Klein's. Here, Bowlby is very outspoken. He once more sharply differentiates his position from that of Melanie Klein, who "invokes a death instinct. I don't. I think it's rubbish."

The first case, presented by Leopolda Pelizzaro, is that of a compulsively self-sufficient woman who joined a revolutionary group. Bowlby congratulates the therapist on her approach, and points out the similarity between the patient and Mrs G. He also commends the therapist for her readiness to carry out a telephone session. At one point he says, "There's a saying, 'We are forced to repeat what we cannot remember'." Here, he forgets to mention that it was Freud who said it repeatedly in his work, for instance in his 1914 paper on technique (Freud, 1914g, p. 150).

Ferruccio then presents the case of a male patient who was sent to boarding school at the age of five. Bowlby surmises that this patient was battered as a baby. He points out that what is missing in the patient's reports are his feelings. He repeats the self-criticism he had already expressed in "Violence in the family": "we professionals have been deplorably ignorant and naive about things that go on in disturbed families. They are much worse than people think. ... Where, in the psychiatric literature, is there any discussion, by psychiatrists treating adult patients, of the consequences of childhood battering?" Since this patient felt like attacking his daughter when she cried, Bowlby speaks of "a tendency for everyone to model their behaviour on that of their parents". I think that, more specifically, what is at play here is identification with the aggressor, first described by Ferenczi (e.g., Ferenczi, 1933), well before Anna Freud (1936), who is generally credited with this notion. This patient was unable to express feelings. In this connection, Bowlby cites Selma Fraiberg and her co-workers (the citation is in the References of the seminar), who "took it upon themselves to express the feelings" that the patients were unable to express. This is known as mediate catharsis.

Finally, there is Milly's presentation of a woman who was very disorganised and made a suicide attempt. In the tape, the presentation is missing and there is only Bowlby's comment, so Milly presents the case again, together with its follow-up. Bowlby says, "There is the possibility of an affective disorder. I have much too little experience of psychotic patients, so I am unqualified to comment." This is a surprising statement, considering Bowlby trained at the Maudsley Hospital (Van Dijken, 1998, p. 68). Bowlby was pessimistic about this patient. Unfortunately, his pessimism turned out to be justified, as Milly states in her report below.

One final comment on the seminar. At present, Bowlby's views have gained wide acceptance in Italy, not so much in psychoanalysis, but more in the teaching of psychology. Since the seminar was attended by many professionals, it might well be that it made some contribution to this change. This is attested by the report by Germana Agnetti and Angelo Barbato.

## My own comments

I now wish to make three comments of my own on the subject of Bowlby and attachment theory.

First, Bowlby's very empathic interest in the impact of separation on small children might well have biographical roots. According to Van Dijken (1998, p. 26), Bowlby's nanny, to whom he was very attached, left when he was four years old. In this connection, there is a poignant passage in Bowlby's theoretical introduction to the seminar, when he speaks of children who are told not to cry. "For example, a child of five whose nanny is leaving is told not to cry because that would make it more difficult for nanny." In this experience, Bowlby was preceded by Freud. In his letters to Fliess of October 1897, Freud (1985, p. 268) reveals his attachment to his nanny and his despair over her departure. It is instructive to compare Freud to Bowlby. Bowlby also lost his nanny when he was a child, but he developed into a warm and caring person, and did not become a detached and authoritarian person like Freud, who advised analysts to "model themselves . . . on the surgeon, who puts aside all his feelings" (Freud, 1912e, p. 115) or to be "opaque . . . like a mirror" (p. 118).

Second, in the last years of his life, Bowlby, as we have seen, was much more aware of the traumatic nature of the experience of many children. This raises the question of the connection between the three phases of a child's reaction to separation, observed by Bowlby in his early work, and the reactions of children to trauma, described in the trauma literature (Herman, 1992, p. 96) and chiefly characterised by dissociation. Within the attachment literature, the description by Mary Main of D-type attachment is a relevant contribution (Main & Hesse, 1990). In *A Secure Base*, Bowlby himself discusses cases of dissociation, which he calls "personality splitting" (Bowlby, 1988b, p. 114). At a theoretical level, he subscribed to the "neodissociative" position of Hilgard (Bowlby, 1980, p. 58), who explicitly goes back to Janet (1898)—the first to introduce the concept of dissociation.

Third, at a higher systemic level, the widespread occurrence of a detached character structure requires reference to the socio-historical dimension. This level is implicit in Bowlby when he says that, if the environment departs too widely from the EEA (the environment of evolutionary adaptedness), pathology will ensue. He discusses this subject in Chapter Four of *Attachment* (Bowlby, 1969). There is some social critique in his work. For instance, on page 2 of *A Secure Base* (Bowlby, 1988b) he says that in the world's richest societies

> man and woman power devoted to the production of material goods counts a plus in all our economic indices. Man and woman power devoted to the production of happy, healthy, and self-reliant children in their own homes does not count at all. We have created a topsy-turvy world.

Erich Fromm's (1941) psychoanalytic social psychology, and in particular his concept of social character, might be relevant here. According to Fromm, every society, acting through the family, tends to mould the character structure most suitable to the perpetuation of that particular society. A detached character structure might be the most suitable for functioning in the aggressive context of capitalist society, notwithstanding its high emotional cost, which is revealed in various forms of individual and social pathology. The origins of capitalism go back to the predatory patriarchal culture that appeared 4–5 thousand years ago and was superimposed on to the original maternal culture, as Riane Eisler describes in *The Chalice and the Blade* (Eisler, 1987). The maternal culture lasted tens of thousands of years. It had a selective advantage, it is a product of biological evolution, and is still present in our genes. As Bowlby says, "Once the criterion in terms of which a system's function is to be considered is population survival, the fact that much behaviour has an altruistic function is no surprise" (Bowlby, 1969, p. 131). The predatory patriarchal culture only arose 4–5 thousand years ago, it is not in our genes, and has to reassert itself at every generation through the violent socialisation of children. A child's loving relationship with the mother is an expression of the innate maternal culture. If a child is traumatised and full of rage, it has been forcibly transferred from the original maternal culture to the superimposed patriarchal culture. These socio-historical factors could be regarded as the *remote* causation of individual and social pathology.

## Further contributions

To begin with, Leopolda Pelizzaro presents the follow-up of her case, in which she confirms the very empathic approach of her presentation at the seminar.

Ferruccio Osimo then gives the follow-up of the case he presented at the seminar.

As indicated above, Emilia Fumagalli presents her case again, which had been omitted in the tapes, and adds the follow-up, which, sadly, confirms the misgivings expressed by Bowlby in the seminar. She now believes the diagnosis could be that of schizoaffective disorder. I might add that in any case the highly disorganised state of the patient implies an original D-type attachment (Main & Hesse, 1990).

Claudia Ferrandes, who looked after the audio recording, describes the emotional quality of Bowlby's communications, and also reports on her personal involvement with the Bowlbys.

Germana Agnetti and Angelo Barbato report that they gave hospitality to Bowlby and his wife Ursula in their own home, and that Germana's mother housed the whole seminar in her large house. In their contribution, they show how, through the seminar, attachment theory was added to the multiple approaches by which they were influenced at the time in Italy, even if it took time for them to reach an integration.

After his own follow-up, Ferruccio Osimo makes a long and important scientific contribution, in which he presents the brief therapy approach of experiential-dynamic therapy (EDT), which he shares with many others. He regards Habib Davanloo, who proposed intensive short-term dynamic psychotherapy (ISTDP), as "the father of all subsequent experiential dynamic models". One feature of EDT is video recording, which provides empirical evidence of the therapeutic work. Osimo describes the various EDT approaches, which all share some common features, while each has some characteristic features of its own. He then goes on to describe three approaches (Fosha, McCullough, and Neborsky) which, in addition to his own, are especially informed by attachment theory. Neborsky, in particular, makes use of Main's adult attachment interview (AAI). Finally, Osimo presents his own approach, designated as intensive experiential–dynamic psychotherapy (IE–DP), which stresses the real relationship with the therapist. After discussing the consistency of IE–DP and attachment theory, Osimo presents a case study, with extended excerpts from the transcripts of four video-recorded sessions, plus a follow-up session. I shall present my own comments on Osimo's contribution in the "Concluding remarks".

## References

American Psychiatric Association (1980). *Diagnostic and Statistical Manual of Mental Disorders* (3rd edn). Washington, DC: American Psychiatric Association.

Arieti, S. & Arieti, J. A. (1977). *Love Can Be Found. A Guide to the Most Desired and Most Elusive Emotion*. New York: Harcourt Brace & Jovanovich.

Arieti, S., & Bemporad, J. R. (1978). *Severe and Mild Depression. The Psychotherapeutic Approach*. New York: Basic Books.

Bacciagaluppi, M. (1984). Some remarks on the Oedipus complex from an ethological point of view. *Journal of the American Academy of Psychoanalysis, 12*: 471–490.

Bacciagaluppi, M. (1985a). Inversion of parent–child relationships: a contribution to attachment theory. *British Journal of Medical Psychology, 58*: 369–373.

Bacciagaluppi, M. (1985b). Ethological aspects of the work of Erich Fromm. *ContemporaryPsychoanalysis, 21*: 156–166.

Bacciagaluppi, M. (1985c). Letter to the Editor. *Academy Forum, 29*(1): 1.

Bacciagaluppi, M. (1987a). Proximate and remote causation of psychopathology in an ethological framework. Paper presented at the "Sociophysiology" Satellite Symposium of the IBRO Second World Congress of Neurosciences, Pécs-Galosfa, Hungary, August 22–25. Unpublished.

Bacciagaluppi, M. (1987b). Report from Hungary. *Academy Forum, 31*(4): 15.

Bacciagaluppi, M. (1989a). Attachment theory as an alternative basis of psychoanalysis. *American Journal of Psychoanalysis, 49*(4): 311–318.

Bacciagaluppi, M. (1989b). The role of aggressiveness in the work of John Bowlby. *Free Associations, 16*: 123–134.

Bacciagaluppi, M. (1993). Fromm's views on narcissism and the self. In: J. Fiscalini & A. L. Grey (Eds.), *Narcissism and the Interpersonal Self* (pp. 91–106). New York: Columbia University Press.

Bacciagaluppi, M. (2012). *Paradigms in Psychoanalysis. An Integration.* London: Karnac.

Bacciagaluppi, M., & Bacciagaluppi Mazza, M. (1982a). The relevance of ethology to interpersonal psychodynamics and to wider social issues. *Journal of the American Academy of Psychoanalysis, 10*: 85-111.

Bacciagaluppi, M., & Bacciagaluppi Mazza, M. (1982b). An Italian commemoration of Silvano Arieti. *Academy Forum, 26*(1): 9–10.

Bemporad, J. R. (1984). From attachment to affiliation. *American Journal of Psychoanalysis, 44*(1): 79–92.

Bischof, N. (1975). A systems approach towards the functional connections of attachment and fear. *Child Development, 46*: 801–817.

Bischof, N. (1985). *Das Rätsel Ödipus. Die biologischen Wurzeln des Urkonfliktes von Intimität und Autonomie.* Munich: Piper.

Bowen, M. (1978). *Family Therapy in Clinical Practice.* New York: Jason Aronson.

Bowlby, J. (1969). *Attachment and Loss, I, Attachment.* New York: Basic Books.

Bowlby, J. (1973). *Attachment and Loss, II, Separation: Anxiety and Anger.* New York: Basic Books.

Bowlby, J. (1974). Attachment theory, separation anxiety, and mourning. In: S. Arieti (Ed.), *American Handbook of Psychiatry* (revised 2nd edn), Vol. 6 (pp. 292–309). New York: Basic Books.

Bowlby, J. (1979). On knowing what you are not supposed to know and feeling what you are supposed to feel. *Canadian Journal of Psychiatry, 24*: 403–408.

Bowlby, J. (1980). *Attachment and Loss, III, Loss: Sadness and Depression.* New York: Basic Books.

Bowlby, J. (1984). Violence in the family as a disorder of the attachment and caregiving systems. *American Journal of Psychoanalysis, 44*: 9–27.

Bowlby, J. (1986). I processi difensivi alla luce della teoria dell'attaccamento. Introduzione al *Workshop* organizzato a Milano il 27–28 aprile 1985 dal gruppo *Ricerca e psicoterapia. Psicoterapia e Scienze Umane, 20*(2): 3–19.

Bowlby, J. (1988a). Foreword. In: Suttie, I. (1935). *The Origins of Love and Hate*. London: Free Association Books, 1988.

Bowlby, J. (1988b). *A Secure Base*. London: Routledge.

Bowlby, J. (1990). *Charles Darwin. A Biography*. London: Hutchinson.

Bowlby, J., Figlio, K., & Young, R. M. (1986). An interview with John Bowlby on the origins and reception of his work. *Free Associations, 6*: 36–64.

Cain, A. C., & Fast, I. (1972). Children's disturbed reactions to parent suicide. In: A. C. Cain (Ed.), *Survivors of Suicide*. Springfield, IL: Thomas.

Durbin, E. F. M., & Bowlby, J. (1939). *Personal Aggressiveness and War*. London: Routledge Kegan Paul [reprinted 1950].

Eisler, R. (1987). *The Chalice and the Blade*. New York: Harper & Row.

Fairbairn, W. R. D. (1940). Schizoid factors in the personality. In: *Psycho-analytic Studies of the Personality*. London: Tavistock/Routledge, 1952.

Ferenczi, S. (1933). Confusion of tongues between the adults and the child. In: S. Ferenczi (1955). *Final Contributions to the Problems and Methods of Psycho-Analysis*. London: Maresfield Reprints, 1980.

Freud, A. (1936). *The Ego and the Mechanisms of Defense*. New York: International Universities Press.

Freud, S. (1912e). Recommendations to physicians practising psycho-analysis. *S.E. 12*: 111–120.

Freud, S. (1914g). Remembering, repeating and working-through (further recommendations on the technique of psycho-analysis II). *S.E. 12*: 147–156.

Freud, S. (1985). *The Complete Letters of Sigmund Freud to Wilhelm Fliess 1887–1904*. Cambridge, MA: The Belknap Press.

Fromm, E. (1941). *Escape from Freedom*. New York: Farrar & Rinehart.

Fromm, E. (1961). *Marx's Concept of Man*. New York: Ungar.

Fromm, E. (1970). *The Crisis of Psychoanalysis. Essays on Freud, Marx and Social Psychology*. New York: Holt, Rinehart & Winston.

Fromm, E. (1973). *The Anatomy of Human Destructiveness*. New York: Holt, Rinehart & Winston.

Fromm, E., & Maccoby, M. (1970). *Social Character in a Mexican Village*. Englewood Cliffs, NJ: Prentice-Hall.

Gedo, J. E. (1979). *Beyond Interpretation. Toward a Revised Theory for Psychoanalysis*. New York: International Universities Press.

Goldberg, J. (Ed.) (1981). *Psychotherapeutic Treatment of Cancer Patients*. New York: Free Press.

Greenberg, M. T., & Mitchell, S. A. (1983). *Object Relations in Psychoanalytic Theory*. Cambridge, MA: Harvard University Press.

Grünbaum, A. (1984). *The Foundations of Psychoanalysis. A Philosophical Critique*. Berkeley, CA: University of California Press.

Guidano, V. F., & Liotti, G. (1983). *Cognitive Processes and Emotional Disorders. A Structural Approach to Psychotherapy*. New York: Guilford Press.

Gut, E. (1989). *Productive and Unproductive Depression. Success or Failure of a Vital Process*. New York: Basic Books.

Heard, D. (1978). From object relations to attachment theory: a basis for family therapy. *British Journal of Medical Psychology, 51*: 67–76.

Herman, J. (1981). *Father–Daughter Incest*. Cambridge, MA: Harvard University Press.

Herman, J. (1992). *Trauma and Recovery*. New York: Basic Books.

Horowitz, M. J. (1979). *States of Mind. Analysis of Change in Psychotherapy*. New York: Plenum.

Janet, P. (1898). *Névroses et idées fixes*. I. Paris: Félix Alcan.

Kernberg, O. F. (1975). *Borderline Conditions and Pathological Narcissism*. New York: Jason Aronson.

Klein, M. (1981). On Mahler's autistic and symbiotic phases: an exposition and evaluation. *Psychoanalysis and Contemporary Thought, 4*: 69–105.

Kohut, H. (1971). *The Analysis of the Self. A Systematic Approach to the Psychoanalytic Treatment of Narcissistic Personality Disorders*. New York: International Universities Press.

Kuhn, T. (1962). *The Structure of Scientific Revolutions*. Chicago, IL: The University of Chicago Press.

Mahler, M. S., Pine, F., & Bergman, A. (1975). *The Psychological Birth of the Human Infant. Symbiosis and Individuation*. New York: Basic Books.

Mahoney, M. J., & Freeman, A. (1985). *Cognition and Psychotherapy*. New York: Plenum.

Main, M., & Hesse, E. (1990). Parents' unresolved traumatic experiences are related to infant disorganization status. In: M. T. Greenberg, D. Cicchetti, & E. M. Cummings (Eds.), *Attachment in the Preschool Years. Theory, Research and Intervention* (pp. 121–160). Chicago, IL: Chicago University Press.

Masson, J. M. (1984). *The Assault on Truth. Masson's Suppression of the Seduction Theory*. Harmondsworth: Penguin.

Miller, A. (1979). *Das Drama des begabten Kindes*. Frankfurt: Suhrkamp. English translation: *The Drama of the Gifted Child and the Search for the True Self*. London: Faber & Faber, 1983.

Minuchin, S. (1974). *Families and Family Therapy*. London: Tavistock.

Peterfreund, E. (1983). *The Process of Psychoanalytic Therapy. Models and Strategies*. Hillsdale, NJ: Analytic Press.

Popper, K. R. (1963). *Conjectures and Refutations: The Growth of Scientific Knowledge*. London: Routledge.

Sander, L. (1977). The regulation of exchange in the infant–caregiver system and some aspects of the context–content relationship. In: M. Lewis & L. Rosenblum (Eds.), *Interaction, Conversation, and the Development of Language* (pp. 133–156). New York: Wiley.

Schecter, D. E. (1978). Attachment, detachment and psychoanalytic therapy. In: E. G. Witenberg (Ed.), *Interpersonal Psychoanalysis: New Directions* (pp. 81–104). New York: Gardner Press.

Scott, J. P. (1958). *Aggression*. Chicago, IL: University of Chicago Press.

Searles, H. (1965). *Collected Papers on Schizophrenia and Related Subjects*. New York: International Universities Press.

Slipp, S. (1973). The symbiotic survival pattern: a relational theory of schizophrenia. *Family Process, 12*: 377–398.

Stern, D. N. (1985). *The Interpersonal World of the Infant. A View from Psychoanalysis and Developmental Psychology*. New York: Basic Books.

Van Dijken, S. (1998). *John Bowlby: His Early Life. A Biographical Journey into the Roots of Attachment Theory*. London: Free Association Books.

Videgård, T. (1983). *The Success and Failure of Primal Therapy. 32 Patients Treated at The Primal Institute (Janov) Viewed in the Perspective of Object-Relations Theory*. Stockholm: Almqvist & Wiksell.

Weiss, R. S. (1975). *Marital Separation*. New York: Basic Books.

Winnicott, D. W. (1960). Ego distortion in terms of true and false self. In: *The Maturational Processes and the Facilitating Environment*. London: Hogarth.

Zuckerman, S. (1932). *The Social Life of Monkeys and Apes*. London: Kegan Paul.

Zuckerman, S. (1982). *Nuclear Illusions and Reality*. London: Collins.

# General discussion

*John Bowlby*

*EF*:   [Briefly introduces Bowlby's basic concepts]

*FO*:   Dr Bowlby will read his paper directly in English. You have a copy. Questions will follow. In the afternoon and tomorrow morning there will be discussions of clinical cases.

*JB*:   [I have already summarised above, in my introduction, this theoretical introduction by Bowlby. Much of it will later be published in *A Secure Base* (Bowlby, 1988b), on the following pages:

p. 33, paragraph 1;
p. 34, paragraph 2;
pp. 68 (starting from paragraph 2) to 70 (paragraph 1);
pp. 101 (starting from last paragraph) to 102;
pp. 106 (starting from paragraph 3) to 109 (paragraph 1)].

Interval

*Question*:   From a scientific point of view, what you say allows us to better understand what we do. From a practical point of view, when we find ourselves in a critical situation, what do we do? I would like to ask you in particular: is it only a question of focusing our attention on particular aspects, or could it be that more constructions should be used?

*JB*:    Your last point—constructions and interpretations. Now, I think our task is to enable a patient to discover within himself, to explore within himself, the feelings and thoughts and experiences he had in his life, and how they are affecting him at present. So, sometimes I put it this way. An interpretation tends to be: "I know. I'm telling you, the patient." "I know more than you." Now, I think my attitude is, "*You* know, I don't." "You are informed about all the things that matter. It's our joint task to explore your own experience and discover it." So, I see myself as a companion in exploration rather than an interpreter. So, in that sense, I think my emphasis is more on the patient discovering than me giving reconstructions.

I think it's very important for us, as analysts, to assist the patient to discover, and at times to make suggestions: "Have you ever thought that perhaps your mother or your father threatened to abandon you?" (to take an example).

Not only are we sometimes suggesting possibilities. I mean, we don't know, but we suggest possibilities. But also, I think, and this is *most* important . . . a patient may be very anxious, and hesitant, and afraid to make a proposal, because he thinks you disagree with him. I think we need to be alert. You see, the more we know about the traumatic events of childhood, the kind of things that might have happened, the more we are able to be useful companions in exploration.

*Question*:    What is the most relevant information to allow to emerge? Does it depend on being accepting towards the patient, namely on a human level, or perhaps also on accepting that it was real-life experiences, and not fantasies, that made the patient ill?

*JB*:    I think it's vital that we respect the real-life experiences which patients report. I think it's vital that we accept them as likely to be valid. But we also have to be accepting, in the sense of providing the patient with a secure base. We have to be the patient's attachment figure. Perhaps I can give an analogy. In so far as patients are telling us about painful, frightening experiences, we have to be a companion who gives them courage.

*Question*:   Traditional psychoanalysis defines repression not as repression of real-life experiences, but of fantasies. In this case, the work of the analyst runs the risk of not succeeding in bringing to consciousness the expression of real facts. It might even be that analysis promotes new pathologies or facilitates the continuation of the old pathology.

*JB*:   Well, you see, I was trained in London, I had a Kleinian training, so I was very familiar with fantasy and phases of development and so on. But my experiences in children's work, in family work, always made it clear to me that real-life experiences are important, and I do believe that it is very adverse for a patient when the analyst rejects, or fails to believe, or give respect to, the recollections that a patient tells us about.

If I may say a word, my experience has been that so many psychiatrists and psychoanalysts who only work with adult patients are ignorant of all the work that has been done in recent years in the field of developmental psychology. During my lecture last night in the university [editor's note: I have no information on this], I was giving a brief sketch of some of the enormous range of knowledge we now have about development and actual experiences. But this range of knowledge is unknown amongst my psychiatric and psychoanalytic colleagues.

*Question*:   You talked about attachment and separation. I would like to have a word from you about dependence, and what you consider the place of dependence is in this continuum between attachment and separation.

*JB*:   Let me say some words about dependence first. Now, in England, the words "dependence", "interdependence", have constantly been used to describe a certain type of behaviour. Now, I think that the word "dependence" in English has a pejorative sense. There is a critical aspect. You should be independent. You see, the concept of attachment is one to be valued. Dependence is a bad thing. Attachment is a good thing. Attachment is something which we value. It is part of human nature. It is to be understood and respected by parents and everyone else. The value which belongs to dependence is adverse. The value which belongs to attachment is favourable.

That's a first point.

The second point is that we are attached to particular people, to particular individuals. Instead, we could be dependent on anyone. We are dependent, for instance, on a shopkeeper for providing us with goods. We are dependent on a taxi driver for getting us somewhere. So, there are many instances when we are dependent on someone else. But, of course, we have no emotional attachment to them, so these are quite different concepts.

*Question*:    [One participant works with drug addicts. He would like to know something more about this relation between dependence and attachment in that particular framework. He gives an example. Somebody becomes attached to somebody else and therefore develops also a dependence, because this other person is the one who gives him the drug, and so there might be these two things together, or perhaps not.]

*JB*:    Well, this is a field in which I have not worked, and I am very diffident about discussing it. My belief is that people become drug addicts because they have left a secure attachment in their family of origin. In the attachments that they make within the drug culture, they are clutching at some sort of attachment which they never really had. It's a substitute for a secure attachment which has been absent from their lives.

*Question*:    I would like to go over some of these points. How do you explain the behaviour of the child when he shows negative attitudes towards the mother? For example, one of the most important behaviours that we see is when a child, separated from the mother, doesn't show any more attachment behaviour. Later, when he goes back home, he does not show attachment behaviour and shows anger.

*JB*:    When he goes home, he may show detachment for a time, and then he shows attachment and anger. I think perhaps I may have confused you. What I was describing in regard to separation in institutions is a distinct theoretical system from what I was describing in the latter part of the paper. As I see it, a small child, of about eighteen months to two and a half years of age, who is in a strange place, with strange people, in an institution, initially cries out and protests. His attachment behaviour, his attachment strivings, are very intense and very strong. He may cry for several days, and then he withdraws in depression and despair. Then, after that, we get detachment. It's a phased process.

Now, as I see it, the detachment that develops, it's like a machine that is so overworked that it breaks down. It's as though there were a safety device that cuts out, when the machine is overworked. During the early days of separation there is a tremendous intensification of attachment behaviour, and that could have adverse physiological effects if it went on forever. And so you get a cutter. And that's the way I see it.

*Question*:    That woman you described was not able to show attachment behaviour towards her analyst because this behaviour was connected with suffering. Does the same occur in the child?

*JB*:    I think we are in agreement. As you say, in the case of the adult patient, we describe the situation that she is afraid to make an attachment because of the pain of expected rejection. That's one way in which we describe the situation. In the case of a small child, say, of eighteen months, it's more difficult to conceptualise, and consequently to put it in a different language. But essentially it's the same thing, as I see it. One is using subjective language and the other is using objective language, but they are two sides of the same coin. We use one language in one situation and a different language in another.

And, of course, when the child becomes re-attached after returning home, he becomes intensely demanding, intensely clinging, exceedingly anxious about being separated again. And constantly angry when he thinks it might happen again. The clinging child is a child who is afraid of separation—separation anxiety.

*Question*:    What about autistic children? Does this happen because the child never had a situation of attachment in his life, he has never experienced it? Or because attachment has brought about so much suffering that he's defending against attachment again?

*JB*:    Well, I believe that the true autistic child is a child who is born with a constitutional disability. I think it's a constitutional condition, initially. Of course, we can describe an autistic child as showing a very defective attachment. An autistic child shows some measure of attachment, but it's a very disturbed version of attachment. I think it's a constitutional problem initially. It can either be made better by wise and affectionate handling, or it can be made much worse by rejection.

Autistic children are very difficult to care for, and consequently they are also rejected, and made much worse by rejection.

*Question*:    Exactly what do you mean by constitutional defects in the case of autistic children?

*JB*:    Well, let me say I am not an expert on autistic children. My belief is that they have either a genetic defect or else brain damage. That's my belief. And I think that a colleague of mine in London, Michael Rutter [editor's note: I cite a later work, Rutter & Rutter, 1993], has written extensively on autistic children, and I have no reason to question his general position.

*Question*:    What is the difference between representational model and internal object?

*JB*:    The term "representational model" I regard as a preferable way of describing what has hitherto been described as an internal object. It describes what the parent has presented to the child. To my mind, "representational model" describes that well, whereas the term "internal object" is impersonal, and doesn't indicate that it's an accurate representation of the way in which that parent has behaved to the child. So, it's a matter of choice of words, as I see it.

*Question*:    Can a positive form of dependence exist, or a negative form of attachment? Or is attachment always positive, and dependence always negative?

*JB*:    These are just words. We have to describe patterns of attachment. A pattern of attachment can be secure, which means that the child is confident and trusting that he will be cared for and will not be abandoned or rejected. A secure attachment means that a child is so confident that his attachment figure is affectionate and encouraging and supportive that he can do all sorts of other things. He doesn't have to worry about it. Now, an anxious attachment is where the individual is so apprehensive that he will be rejected, or abandoned, or that something will go wrong, that he has to be very clinging and demanding. So, we are talking about patterns of attachment, some of which are consistent with favourable personality development, and others are inconsistent with favourable personality development and lead to anxiety, on the one hand – an anxious and clinging type of behaviour – or, alternatively, to the kind of narcissistic personality that I was describing in this patient.

*Question*: By using different terms you are describing concepts that are similar to those of the Kleinian framework. For instance, when you say anxious attachment, or abandonment, the substance is more or less the same.

*JB*: Well, I think the conceptual framework of attachment theory is very different to Melanie Klein's. We are, of course, studying the same problems, and consequently, there are areas that overlap, naturally. But, I mean, to take an example, Melanie Klein invokes a death instinct. I don't. I think it's rubbish. Melanie Klein invokes a paranoid–schizoid position in early life. I don't. So, there are so many differences in the conceptual framework that I think it's misleading to suppose that the two are in some ways similar. We are dealing with the same problems, but in fact we are looking at them from quite different perspectives.

*Question*: I just want to put a clinical question. There are several psychoanalysts, especially American, who think that it is better to have five sessions per week. You think that only two or three are enough, maybe also one session per week.

*JB*: Well, it's an empirical question, and until systematic studies have been made of these alternative ways of treating patients, no one is in a position to be confident of which is best, or which is best for certain patients. So, I see it as an entirely empirical issue, needing research. I'm open-minded, but I think that to claim that five times a week is best is unproven.

*Question*: How do you think it is possible to test the possibility of which is the best?

*JB*: Well, it's terribly difficult. This is why it's not been done. I think we shall have to approach it from a new viewpoint. To take an example, let's use Mrs G, the patient I was describing as an illustration. Now, as I see it, the analysis of Mrs G followed a predictable and intelligible sequence. I think one could use, in my terms, the process of analysis of Mrs G as predictable and coherent. First of all, we have to study a number of patients and to recall whether or not, when they are treated in a particular way, the changes that occur are of the same kind and in the same sequence. That's one proposition. Then, of course, we have to determine, if that is the case, how can we best help the patient to go through that process best: by seeing him or her five times for fifty minutes in a week, or, let us say, for five hours on one day, which is possible. I believe that long sessions can be very productive, especially in that type of patient. So, it's an empirical issue.

*Question*:   Is there a link, as Malan maintains, between selection criteria, the technique employed, and predictable results?

*JB*: I would expect that.

# First case presentation: Medusa the revolutionary

*Leopolda Pelizzaro*

T his woman patient says of herself that she was "a different child". Her nannies never punished her. When she was small, she was very proud of being able to make her parents feel better. She always saw herself as being very attractive, different from other children. She sees the years of her childhood and adolescence as being special. "I felt more mature than the others. And I didn't like it at all when my friends cried. Around the age of twelve I started having very strange sensations. At times I felt my body didn't belong to me." She rationalises everything by saying, "I have always been a special girl." In therapy she emerges as a child who was always alone. She used to play with her dolls, cutting herself off from everyone. "I lived in a world of my own, where I was the only one to understand every-body else and my own self."

She goes to High School, then studies medicine. At the same time, she joins a large revolutionary group that uses violence to try to change society. She becomes the partner of one of the leaders, then marries him. This is one of the happiest periods of her life. Into this violent context she puts all the rage and hatred she feels towards everyone.

The marriage changes things somewhat. With her husband, she takes on the role of [one] who does everything. She is a mother to him, a wife, she does everything in the house, she works as a GP, and the husband depends exclusively on her. She and her husband are the only members of the group who have not undergone judicial proceedings.

The first problems arise when she wants a child. Her husband is against it, but she compels him, becomes pregnant, and a girl is born, who is now seven years old. She remembers her relationship with her new-born child as the happiest period in her life.

Further problems arise when the child starts being more autonomous and goes to nursery school. The patient starts feeling bad. Problems with the husband arise again. At the same time, she feels the need to be able to allow herself not to cope with everything. "I wanted to let myself go somewhat." Her need to be cared for was in contrast to the part of her that wanted to do everything and asked for nothing. The husband starts reproaching her for not being as she used to be: the strong one, the one who did everything. He starts to distance himself. However, he does not allow her to find other solutions. The patient starts to feel very bad. She isolates herself, she starts not eating, and she stays indoors.

She meets a colleague, has an affair with him, gets pregnant, then has an abortion.

She cannot stand the idea of separating from the husband. She wishes to have another child. Once more, she asserts herself. She gets pregnant, and once more feels very bad. "I was afraid I would not be able to give to this child what I had given to the first one." She decides to have an abortion.

After the abortion, she starts feeling very bad again. She feels disgusting. She starts isolating herself again, stays indoors, and feels disorientated. The husband says, "You are no good, you are no longer the woman you used to be." She attempts suicide by taking many pills.

For the first time in her life, she turns to a psychiatrist, who advises analysis. That's how she came to me.

In the therapeutic relationship, her need to be taken care of emerges. At the same time, she denies this need, for fear of entrusting herself to someone who may leave her and make her suffer, and above all, who is not omnipotent and does not save her from unwanted feelings.

For a long time she devalues me. She says I do not help her enough. She feels humiliated. All this reminds her of her feeling of impotence when she had to depend on her parents. She associates this to her hospitalisation, when she was strapped to the bed.

Her need to be taken care of cannot coexist with feelings of rage and hostility, which are directed at her husband. She needs to protect me from these feelings.

Lately, she has expressed her disappointment because the analysis is not a total reconstruction but only a series of partial reconstructions. She starts missing sessions and having suicidal ideas. She also has episodes of manic excitement.

In the past month, after an attempt at a phone session, she speaks of the terror, but also of the fascination, of looking at herself in the mirror.

Here are the three latest sessions. In a telephone session, she says she feels helped by me. She recalls having been scalded by boiling water when she was a child. In the hospital, she was treated with a physiological method. After that, she never cried any more. She is fascinated by the prospect of being restored to life, but fears she is deceiving herself. Since she has been feeling better, she has been able to separate from her husband. She still has difficulty in entrusting herself to me. She feels angry at having to depend. She can't hate someone she loves, just as in the hospital she couldn't hate the physicians who gave her pain but also saved her. She still has a tendency to devalue me, but this relationship is the only one in which she feels understood. In the last session, she expresses pain at confronting what she might have been and was unable to be.

*Question*: To what extent is it possible and advisable to try to bring the patient to face the reality of painful real-life experience?

# Discussion of first case presentation

*John Bowlby*

L et me make a few remarks.

First, I want to congratulate the therapist for the therapeutic approach which is adopted and the progress that the patient has already made. Plainly, there is still a long way to go, but none the less I think it's a very good beginning.

This patient is, I think, a classical example of what Winnicott would call "false self". The patient, of course, has a great deal in common with the patient I described this morning, Mrs G.

Referring to the history, I think it is very striking. She became compulsively self-sufficient. She's very proud to remember that she always cheered her parents up. She considers herself as different from other people. That's a very classical way of describing self-sufficiency.

Now, I would conjecture that her parents did not like her crying. I think her parents wished her to appear a happy child, and they were not agreeable to her being distressed and unhappy. So, she grows up to be this prematurely adult child, self-sufficient, successful at school and in medicine. It's all quite classical. And she avoids personal relationships, initially, by joining the revolutionary group and engaging in political activities, to get away from private feelings.

The personal relations are what activate all her repressed feelings. She remembers her relation with her daughter as the best in her life. Now, this is the first time, I think, she's allowed herself to feel affection and attachment, and I suspect that she inverted the relationship with her daughter. This is a conjecture. What makes me feel that is her distress when the daughter starts nursery school. And, of course, on the one hand, she explains that she wants to relax, and all her life has been constructed on doing everything for herself. She does it all. But, when she wishes to relax, and she wishes other people to care for her, then of course she feels she is a vulnerable person, especially when she wants other people to care for her. Now, the telephone session which you had with her, strikes me as having been very valuable. She hadn't expected you to agree. She asked, "Am I disturbing you?" She doesn't expect attention, she doesn't expect someone to care for her and to take trouble. You showed yourself to be accessible, and also responsive and helpful, which is not what she expected. Of course, as you say, she's very afraid to make an attachment to you. She makes it, and then she withdraws again. She values you, and then she has to disparage you because she doesn't want to get too close. And, as you see, she's very afraid that the more strongly she is attached to you, the more angry she will be with you when you are not available.

I think that's all I have to say, and I hope others will join the discussion.

*Question*:   [There is a long discussion, difficult to make out, once more concerning attachment and dependence.]

*JB*:   In her childhood, she repressed or defended against being attached to anyone. She became self-sufficient, just as Mrs G. She was afraid to express any distress, or desire for care, or sympathy, or comfort. She had to be special, very mature, she was critical of other children crying. All that was something she distanced herself from. She had to be the cheerful one, she couldn't express her distress. So, she grew up without attachments, as a compulsive, emotionally self-sufficient person. But, during therapy, she begins to wish for her therapist to care for her, to attend to her, and she would like to express a wish for care and to seek comfort. But she's very frightened of doing so, and when she telephones you expects you to turn off. Her representational model of an attachment figure is one who dislikes crying, dislikes distress, and expects her to be happy and independent. So, that is the representational model she brings to the therapeutic relationship, which is why she does not expect sympathy from you, and does not expect you to have time for her.

*Question*:   [There is another long discussion among the participants, difficult to make out.]

*JB*:   Well, clearly, the patient, who is just beginning to trust the therapist enough to become attached, is very uncertain still. But the patient feels that, if she can't make an attachment to her therapist, it would be better to commit suicide. I think that's quite a natural, intelligible reaction. Now, inevitably, any psychotherapist is worried when patients talk a lot about suicide. But one can't pretend one's not worried when one is. I think you have to be honest. So, there's no simple answer to that situation.

I would like to say something about dependency. Now, if we use the word "dependency", if we say "This patient is becoming dependent", then you start using the word "regressive" and suggesting that this is something that is infantile. All those are associated with the word "dependency".

If we use the word "attachment", we see it as progress, not regression, as progress towards a normal state of interpersonal relations. And I think this is a very big difference in outlook.

I think that we have gradually to help our patients confront the real experiences they had in their lives. There's a saying, "We are forced to repeat what we cannot remember", and I think that in order to enable patients to put the past in the past and face the future afresh, we have to help them, so far as we can see, to look at what really did happen in their early life. But this has to be slow, and we can't . . . I believe it's unwise to force the pace, to push.

*Question*:   I have the impression that this patient is playing a very dangerous game, at various levels: in her relationships, and by throwing bombs as a revolutionary. She seems to be emotionally linked with the therapist, but she also has this problem of looking at herself in the mirror, and the fear of finding herself ugly, especially if she should remain without the therapist. Therefore, the threat of separation brings about sensations of not liking herself. Is it possible that re-enacting this pathology, this kind of attachment brings about a further difficulty in accepting herself as she is?

*JB*:   I think she has great difficulties to start with. I don't think the therapy makes it more difficult. And I think that the very fact that the therapist is able to accept her and demonstrates that she can treat her with attention and respect and be accessible and helpful, so far as it is possible, may in due course enable this patient to see herself in a more favourable way. So, I don't see that this is a problem.

*Question*:   I think there is a misleading idea of reparation in the patient. It is linked with explosions, bombs, terrorism, revolution, as though reparation could be brought about only by magical, or manic means, as, for instance, the reconstruction of her skin. So, in a way, she seems to be compulsively attempting to make something explode in her relationship with the therapist, in order to bring about this peculiar kind of reparation which can only follow on an explosion.

*LP*:   [The patient's therapist answers that she doesn't think that what is going on in the therapy is something particularly magical, but that what she is trying to do is to show the patient that she can feel well through little things, and not only through big explosions.]

*JB*:   Well, I think this patient will only be able to fend for herself and deal with the world when she has a secure attachment and she can trust somebody, and I think that the way her therapist is responding to the patient is very helpful. So, I'm afraid that the kind of speculations which the other participant has made are not to my taste. I think you are wearing a pair of spectacles which are different from mine.

*Question*:   The patient had a severe trauma in childhood. She was traumatised by scalding. Another thing is that the patient is now very depressed and has suicidal ideation. Is it possible that she had the same feelings in childhood? The problem was the way she dealt with the trauma. Maybe, the parents were unable to work through the mourning process of that trauma, unable to acknowledge the suffering, and prevented the patient from suffering. The parents taught her to accept everything. She now tries to compensate by saving the world. Until now, she had not found anybody who could accept her suffering when she was scalded. The mirror could mean the wish to be accepted as she really is by her parents, by parents who could accept her suffering when she was scalded.

*JB*:   I find myself very much in agreement with what has been said on this patient. I think this patient's parents found it difficult to accept that a disaster had occurred to their daughter. It is possible that they felt very guilty when this child was scalded, and so they were additionally unwilling to recognise the terrible distress that their daughter was in. As you say, I think they could not sympathise or empathise with her distress and her crying, and it was only when this child put on a brave front that she was acceptable to her parents, and so she had to develop this false self, when she was so special and mature, and was contemptuous of the other children crying. She had to distance herself from anything of that sort. And I think it is the distressed, crying, comfort-seeking aspect of herself which she doesn't expect the therapist to accept.

*Question*:   Is this a distorted perception of reality induced by parents and an encouragement to see them as different from what they are?

*JB*:   Yes, exactly so. As I see it, her parents didn't like her when she was crying and distressed. Her parents insisted that she should be a happy child: she always cheered up her parents; it was her job to be happy and to cancel their own distress about the accident.

*Question*:   [difficult to decipher]

*JB*:   I'm very glad you made that point, because I entirely agree with you. It is only within an increasingly trusting relationship with the therapist that the patient was able to recall both the events and her feelings, her distress, the depression. In the hospital setting this child was sparingly visible. This was depression. It all had to be hidden behind a happy mask.

*Question*:   If detachment is a defence, the analyst's job is to make feelings emerge.

*JB*:   Yes, that is the way I see it. I think with a patient such as this one, she did not trust anyone to be sympathetic. The therapist's job is to be consistent, reliable, sensitive, attentive, and responsive, something a patient of this sort had never had before.

*Question*:   There may be two types of separation, actual and possible. When parents forbid something, are they imposing separation?

*JB*:   I don't see it that way. I think there are real separations and there are threats to separate. That is very important, and more frequent. But frustrating a child is not separation.

*Question*:   If you tell a child: if you touch the fire you will be burned?

*JB*:   That's a statement of fact.

Interval

# Second case presentation: the boarding school boy

*Ferruccio Osimo*

[This is a thirty-year old man who was referred to FO two years ago. He comes twice a week. At one time, the patient missed two sessions because of the Easter holidays, and then he missed a third session because of health problems. In the first half of the next session, he was very angry because he wanted to recoup the missed sessions, but that was not possible for the therapist; in the second half, he associated to separating from the family because of being sent to boarding school. At the next session, he had forgotten everything.]

John Bowlby with Ferruccio Osimo.

# Discussion of second case presentation

*John Bowlby*

T here is a great deal of material here. I would like to ask one or two questions first. When he was angry, you refer to homicidal fantasies.

*FO*:  He had a dream provoked by a film in which SS soldiers are holding a child by the feet and banging his head against a wall. When he got home, his child was crying and he was afraid of doing the same thing to her.

*JB*:  It's very striking that when his daughter was crying he felt like attacking her. That makes me think that this man was battered as a baby. It's what you expect: a child who has been physically assaulted by parents . . . it particularly happens when a child is crying, parents are angry and physically assaultive. Because of a tendency for everyone to model their behaviour on that of their parents, when his daughter cries, he feels hostile.

Now, you said earlier, "His mother appears very seldom in his material." She's described as being completely subdued by the father, and a rather unempathic woman. I am always interested if a patient talks only about mother, then I ask, "What about father?" When he talks about father, I ask, "What about mother?" And I feel that this man's problems have quite as much to do with mother as with father, and probably more so. This is supported by the material that comes out in the second dream. "I'm walking hand in hand with my daughter when a dog starts running after me until he nearly bites me. At that point, a woman catches the dog's mouth with her two hands and twists it like this, and the dog shuts up." Well now, that is associated with his mother twisting the child's mouth in order to shut him up from crying, and this is something mother did.

So, my intuitive understanding of the dream is that the dog is his own angry self at being sent away to the boarding school, dismissed from home, and his mother being unable to bear his crying. I think that whenever he cried, she beat him up, and when she beat him up, she had to stop his crying by holding his mouth.

You see, it's . . . Why was he sent away from home at the age of five? It's unusual. Did the social workers intervene because he was being maltreated at home? Is that possible?

*FO*:   No, he was sent to the boarding school immediately after the birth of his brother, because that was the custom there.

*JB*:   It would appear that, even before he went to boarding school, his relations with his mother were not happy. He recalls an occasion when he was left alone in the house, and was left with the cardboard and needle, and he concentrated a lot on the cardboard, not to think of his mother.

Another point I want to raise is that one of his older sisters died from cancer when the patient was sixteen. Now, I wonder whether this elder sister might have been something of a mother substitute, if his relation with his own mother was not very warm. The elder sister may have had a special significance, so when she died it was a traumatic experience.

*FO*:   The sister came back about one year before dying. She used to help him out with his homework.

Interval

*FO*:   [FO recalls the case discussed on the previous day, and especially the patient's amnesia concerning his two experiences of separation.]

*JB:*   I don't know the answers. But I want to bring out a point which I think there is the danger of our neglecting. We have a lot of information now about small children separated from parents and their behaviour on their return home, when they are very demanding, distressed, and, of course, angry with a parent who shows any sign of abandoning them again. Now, how do these reactions develop in early childhood? Now, a very great deal turns on how the parent reacts, how the parent treats the child at this point. A parent may be sympathetic, understanding, doing his best to comfort the child, recognise that the child is very anxious, and do everything possible to comfort and reassure. It takes time, hard work, but in due course the child becomes more reassured and his attachment becomes secure once again. Now, the problem is that if the child is demanding, the parent punishes him. The more he cries, the more the parent is angry with him. Now, that is when the psychopathology becomes entrenched. So, much turns on how much the child's disturbed behaviour, disturbed emotions, are treated in the weeks and months after the traumatic separation.

Now, in this case, there is evidence that a child who cries is treated adversely. There's two kinds of evidence in this case: one is the story that comes out in the second dream about the dog and how the woman catches the dog's mouth with her two hands and twists it like this to shut the dog up, and that leads to the association that his mother used to seize his mouth to shut him up. So, that's one clear source of evidence that a crying child was unwelcome to mother, who, instead of comforting the child, behaved in this way. The other source of evidence is indirect. Now, I asked Dr Osimo what his homicidal fantasies were, in what circumstances, and directed towards whom. Dr Osimo told us that when his daughter was crying, he felt homicidal towards her. Now, that, to me, again is evidence that an individual who as a child was adversely treated when he was crying, bashed, battered, is disposed to do the same to his own child. So, I feel very confident that in this particular case this patient was very unsympathetically and hostilely treated by a parent when he was upset, distressed and crying.

Now, this leads me to suppose that when—I'm coming back to the treatment—just tell us, what were the feelings he was expressing in the first sessions after separation? Sad, unhappy, angry?

*FO*:   Well, he felt enraged, because . . . the first thing he said was to ask me for some compensatory sessions. After I told him I couldn't, he felt angry and teased by how I sometimes say "yes" and sometimes say "no".

*JB*:   Later in that same session, he was aware of his distress about separation.

*FO*:   He was able to see the similarity between his anger at me and his past separation, but I don't think he was fully in touch with his feelings. I felt as though he made a sort of cognitive report.

*JB*:   Now, what do we have in this situation? This is intellectual cognitive recognition that there is a similarity between the experience of the recent holiday break and the experience when as a child he was sent to boarding school. What is missing are his feelings.

Now, here I'm very much influenced by the paper by Selma Fraiberg, Shapiro, and Adelson [editor's note: actually, Fraiberg, Adelson, & Shapiro]. They wrote a very interesting paper in the *Journal of the American Academy of Child Psychiatry* in 1974 [editor's note: actually, 1975]. The title is "Ghosts in the nursery". It is, in fact, a very valuable description of their work with two mothers, one of whom neglected a baby, and the other of whom was in danger of battering the baby

Now, each of these mothers had had a very traumatic childhood, and each of the mothers could describe in some detail all the horrible events that had occurred in her childhood. But what they could not express were the feelings aroused by those events. So, we have the same situation here. He can recall events, but can't express the feelings. Now, the technique that these workers used was as follows: they took it upon themselves to express the feelings that those women had felt. "That was a dreadful thing to happen. You must have felt upset, miserable, and wanting comfort, and there was no one there to help you; and perhaps your mother, or your father, would have slapped you, if you had cried." So, they entered into the situation, and they expressed all the feelings which they were confident the women would have had as girls, and showed that they understood and sympathised: an active technique.

Yes, I think, to some degree, his discussion of the compensatory session was a diversion. It was an opportunity to wrangle with you, rather than to deal with the distress of separation. Somebody who's had the kind of experiences that this patient I'm sure had as a child feels that a separation is not just a seven-day break, but is an opportunity to reject the therapist better. So, my belief is, you see, that when he returned he was totally unaware of the distress and sadness and depression that he felt as a child, but he also believed that you would be totally unsympathetic to any experience of distress. I emphasise distress because distress is just as important as anger. Distress searches for comfort.

*FO*:   It is important to deal with separation, but it is also important to be empathic. Not giving the compensatory session might have been too rigid.

*JB*:   I think in a situation of this sort you can't do the right thing. My own view is that, if one can give a compensatory session, one should. If one can't, one can't. I don't think the patient benefits from being deprived of a session. If you give them too little they will never expect anything, if you give them a little more they come to expect everything. So, you've always got this problem: either the patient shuts you out, or they are more expectant than you can give. This is the problem which you have. I think that the question of compensatory sessions is not really important. I think the important thing is to deal with the distress about the separation and the expectation that the analyst will be hostile and unsympathetic. I think this man is confident that you will be angry with him and punish him if he expresses himself.

*Question*:   Maybe FO is overemphasising the issue of the compensatory sessions. Maybe he is motivated by something unconscious in himself.

*JB*:   I don't know (laughs).

*Question*:   [There are two issues here. One is linked with the compensatory sessions. The participant wonders if therapy must be only a review of real past experiences, or if it is also based on an interpersonal relationship, that may be a recovery of cognitive experiences. The other point is, if those were real-life experiences. Some patients tend to speak in terms of fantasies.]

*JB*:   Let's take one at a time. Let's take a patient who can talk about fantasies but cannot talk about real-life experiences. One has to be aware that the real experiences must have been painful and also unsympathetically treated by parents during childhood. And I think one has to indicate that one understands first of all that they were very painful experiences and, secondly, no one ever sympathised with them, but their distress was treated with hostility and lack of sympathy. It's only by indicating that one can empathise, one does understand, that they can gain courage to refer to them. That's one side of it. In the case of individuals who can give you detailed accounts of real-life events, as this man can, he doesn't give you the feeling. Now, here, it's our task to indicate that we understand the feelings, and we also know that he does not expect those feelings to be treated with understanding or sympathy.

I want to say this about this man reporting so many traumatic experiences in childhoood. Now, I believe, we professionals have been deplorably ignorant and naïve about things that do go on in disturbed families. They are much worse than people think. Let me give you an example. Thanks to the work of paediatricians such as Kempe, and Helfer [editor's note: the exact reference is: Helfer & Kempe, 1968], we know that some children are battered. We know, too, something about the development of these children. They develop into very anti-social, difficult, violent characters. That's all well documented. Therefore, in our clinical practice, we meet with individuals who had that experience. Now, where, in the psychiatric literature, is there any discussion, by psychiatrists treating adult patients, of the consequences of childhood battering? I know no paper in the whole literature which discusses this problem, and yet it must be done.

*FO*:    [FO goes back to his case, already reported, in which the patient, after a session in which he discussed three previous missed sessions, completely forgot the fourth session.]

*JB*:    He wants to be accepted, but he has no confidence that you will understand. So, to avoid being rejected, he has a battle with you. Anger is important, but it is only half the story. The depression and the desire for comfort is just as important, but tends to be omitted. Anger is only part of the problem. The other half is his desire for comfort, understanding, and his expectation of being rejected. I think that's more fundamental.

# Third case presentation: the case of Adriana

*Emilia Fumagalli*

driana's parents had six children, three male and three female. Of special importance for Adriana were the eldest, Gino, and the youngest, also a male. Adriana was one of the intermediate children. She was sexually abused by Gino between the ages of three and fifteen. When she was an adolescent, the parents separated. Adriana then oscillated between staying with the mother and staying with friends. Gino remained living with his father.

Gino was hospitalised several times with the diagnosis of schizophrenia. In 1978, a law was passed in Italy to close mental hospitals and replace them with outpatient clinics. After the mental hospitals were closed, Gino refused to go to the outpatient clinic and refused to take drugs. The clinic was contacted by the father, and home visits were arranged. I am a psychotherapist, and I used to visit the patient at home, together with a psychiatrist. These visits used to make us anxious. Gino was verbally aggressive, very long-winded and declaiming. At times, we hoped he wouldn't open the door.

Gino eventually committed suicide by throwing himself out of a window. After his suicide, Adriana went to live with her father and started coming to the outpatient clinic. She was around thirty. At the clinic she, too, was diagnosed as schizophrenic and given Haloperidol. I used to interview her once a week.

Whereas Gino was rejecting, Adriana was emotionally involved. Her behaviour was highly impulsive and included suicide attempts, chance love affairs, and abortions. Her psychiatrist and I at times felt exhausted. Her rapid mood changes made Bowlby think of an affective disorder. At present, I would rather make a diagnosis of schizoaffective disorder, because of the presence of positive schizophrenic symptoms (hallucinations). The notion of schizoaffective disorder was only introduced into the *DSM* in 1980, and Bowlby might not have been familiar with it.

Adriana was very good-looking. She knew it, and used her good looks to seduce men. She was looking for a secure attachment, but she actually found men who either exploited her or were even weaker than she was. Once she told me, "I would like to have a normal life, with a job and a family, or at least one of these two things."

There was one dramatic incident that was commented on by Bowlby. After having been rejected by a man, Adriana went to the cemetery where her brother was buried, taking various types of drug with her. At closing time, she escaped attention, stayed in the cemetery, and took all the drugs. The next morning, she was found in a comatose state. She survived because it was winter and the cold had induced hypothermia. I went to see her in the intensive care unit.

Unfortunately, Bowlby's pessimism was justified. Some time after the seminar, Adriana committed suicide by throwing herself out of the same window as the brother. Some days before, she had been told that her youngest brother, who lived with the mother and whom she had tried to protect, had been hospitalised in a psychiatric unit for the first time. Maybe this event made her feel that there was a fate she could not escape.

I wrote on the cover of her file, "As therapists, we looked after Adriana for eight years. At the end, the adverse events of her life and her illness prevailed."

I now ask myself what else we could have done. In those days, an integrated therapeutic approach and therapeutic communities were lacking in Italy. Adriana's case led me to undertake training in family therapy and to treat severe cases with conjoint individual and family therapy.

In this case, there is an important link with attachment theory. Both the suicide attempt at the cemetery and the final suicide reveal a pathological attachment to the abusive brother, whom she had to follow also in death. There is a connection with the brother also in the affairs with men who exploited her, or who were weaker than she was. Bowlby pointed out that when the attachment figure is also the one who elicits fear, the child, paradoxically, clings all the more (Bowlby, 1969, pp. 215–216, 1973, p. 91).

I learned much from Adriana, and her memory still moves me.

# Discussion of third case presentation

*John Bowlby*

[As has been indicated already, the case is missing in the tapes, and EF has presented her case once more, above, together with the follow-up.]

*JB*:   EF is very courageous in dealing with this patient. At the end of your paper, you ask two questions. You refer to the fact that on the first occasion, during your holiday, this patient reacted with disorganisation and with erotomanic delusion, but, on the second occasion, she reacted with a suicide attempt in a very lucid manner. Well, I wonder, would it not be correct to regard her planned suicide attempt as a substantial progress. Now, that may seem paradoxical, but it seems to me that on this occasion she was able to take a planned step. Formerly, she collapsed into a chaotic psychological condition. On this occasion, it was a perfectly organised attempt. It was obviously serious, I'm not saying it wasn't serious. But I would think that, paradoxically, this may well be counted as progress. Of course, she says, like many others, that what she wants is a settled family home. She's had a very disorganised life. I'm sure she had no secure attachment. Her childhood was obviously very unsatisfactory. The second point is the question [of] how one treats a patient. Is it possible to treat this patient on an outpatient service, or would the psychotherapy be more effective if done in a protective ambience? I'm not sure if it would be practical. She wouldn't stay. The risk of this woman committing suicide is high. I think one has to accept that. The only thing is to do your best. But I think that her relationship to you is valuable. The difficulty with a patient of this sort is that the disorganisation of her life is so great that, in order to assist her, you need a very, very long time. I believe that if it were possible for you, you could help her over a long, long period. But the practical problems are enormous. Progress is a small step movement towards greater personality integration.

Even when she attempts suicide, she does so in the cemetery, at her brother's grave, she is joining her brother.

*EF*:    What strikes me in this patient are her rapid changes.

*JB*:    I agree. There is the possibility of an affective disorder. I have much too little experience of psychotic patients, so I am unqualified to comment. I believe that psychotherapy is no worse than other treatments. It may be that, together with psychotropic drugs, it might be useful, but it's outside my experience. After all, this suicide attempt was a direct reaction to the parody of her relationship with this man, after she'd had hopes with this thirty-year-old man that that might develop after he had rejected her; it's a direct response to separation. Her situation is dreadfully frightening. That is her condition in life. First of all, she has no relationships which are stable, and secondly, of course, she has such a disturbed personality that she is incapable of breaking relationships. She is isolated. That's her state in life.

*EF*:    She told me: "My life is a failure". I was about to say, "It's true", but I merely added, "Let's see what we can do."

*JB*:    That would have been a good answer.

# Conclusion of the seminar

*FO:* Speaking of separation, the time has come for us to separate. Dr Bowlby has shown us of what fundamental importance attachment is in humans, and how, in order to understand pathology, it is necessary to investigate real-life events. Thank you very much, Dr Bowlby.

*JB:* Thank you all. I've enjoyed it.

## References

Fraiberg, S., Adelson, E., & Shapiro, V. (1975). Ghosts in the nursery: a psychoanalytic approach to the problems of impaired infant–mother relationships. *Journal of the American Academy of Child Psychiatry, 14:* 387–421.

Helfer, E., & Kempe, C. H. (Eds.) (1968). *The Battered Child.* Chicago, IL: University of Chicago Press.

Rutter, M., & Rutter, M. (1993). *Developing Minds. Challenge and Continuity Across the Life Span.* New York: Basic Books.

Winnicott, D. W. (1960). Ego distortion in terms of true and false self. In: *The Maturational Processes and the Facilitating Environment.* London: Hogarth, 1965.

# Follow-up of first case presented

*Leopolda Pelizzaro*

T reatment continued for three more years. What I remember is the effort required to stand up to the terror, the fury, and the great mental suffering which the patient began to present.

The pain was due to loss and the unreal possibility of a total "reconstruction" of her body.

Her very great anger was directed at me. She used to scream at me and at the whole world. She would say things like "You treat me like a skinned horse". This sentence stuck in my mind because of the vehemence, the despair, and the hatred it expressed. She felt that way, but this had really happened when, as a little girl, the bandages had been removed. The real trauma re-emerged, and the therapist was there to share it. She said this on the strength of the attachment relationship that we had laboriously built up.

One day, after expressing this fury, she burst into tears. That was unforgettable, as well as my own reaction. The patient stood up screaming and crying desperately, then she crouched on the floor. I got up and embraced her, trying to calm her that way rather than through interpretations. I believe my containing her physically, instead of running away, was very therapeutic. For the first time, unlike her parental figures, there was someone who stayed with her, who was not afraid of seeing and hearing a terrified child, "mad with pain", full of fury that she could at last express and no longer displace on to politics and through terrorist groups.

After a while, vital projects appeared: she attended tango lessons (whereas previously she could not stand being embraced), she met a man, fell in love with him, and shared many small but pleasant things with him.

Therapy terminated with her acknowledging her wish to be loved and allowing her friends and new boyfriend to touch her. She has become much more sensitive to the pain of her patients, and has repeatedly co-operated fully with those who could help her. She had also thought of enrolling in the study of psychology.

After the end of treatment, for some years we met around Christmas "as if not to forget", as she would say. I remember she no longer looked defiant, was pleased with her emotional situation, and, above all, was much more tolerant of her own limits and her aggressiveness, which she no longer projected outside.

# Follow-up of second case presented

*Ferruccio Osimo*

A fter the supervision with John Bowlby at the seminar, I strove to handle the patient's rage, triggered by the missed sessions, in a different way. I managed to leave behind the argumentative and demanding atmosphere by shifting our attention to the patient's perception of the therapist as a real person, and to my perception of him as a real person. This was effective in enabling us to continue therapy for another four months and come to an agreed conclusion of treatment. In terms of therapeutic outcome, the patient was able to experience some trust in the therapist and some affection for him, which was certainly a healing experience for him. There are, however, two main reservations: (1) the termination date was decided because of an external event, the patient's move with his family to another town; (2) according to the therapist's perception, the patient did not completely renounce his essentially distrustful attitude, at least not until the end of treatment. Since we do not have any after-termination data, we do not know if the partial character change that was achieved went any further, came to a halt or, in the worst hypothesis, was undone. With hindsight, I believe that, if the handling of the patient's character defences had been effective enough to make him renounce his attitude of distancing and distrust, this would have paved the way to a full emotional experiencing. This, in turn, might have been worked through in the relationship with the therapist, further promoting the adaptive change and making it permanent.

# Surprisingly simple: planning the seminar

*Claudia Ferrandes*

There was much excitement when we started meeting to plan the seminar. Angelo, Ferruccio, Germana, Milly, and I were much taken by the magnitude of the task. For all of us, this was the first time we had organised a scientific event at an international level, and everything had to run smoothly. It is, therefore, not surprising that in the course of some of the preparatory meetings there should have been some tension. Thinking back, I believe our fresh minds and our inexperience eventually contributed to the success of the enterprise. I hope this brief record of recollections and images reflects my feeling of having lived through, with much participation, a highly significant experience, that at the same time was surprisingly simple. I believe this also depended on John Bowlby's own personality. Also thanks to the presence of his wife Ursula and to their strong bond, he succeeded in offering us, in addition to his theory, a tangible example of secure attachment.

Among the tasks that had been entrusted to me was that of dealing with the audio recording, which involved my always being present and turning or replacing the cassettes every forty-five minutes. In the supervision of cases and the discussions, I remember being struck by the contrast between the complex and, at times, lengthy comments on the part of the participants, on the one hand, and the extreme simplicity of Bowlby's comments, on the other. Because of my work, I was constantly in touch with people with eating disorders who mostly had scant mentalisation. The emotional and simple communications of this great scholar were of great value to me and helped me in my daily commitment to communicate with patients. Now it seems obvious. Of course, it is essential to *feel* attachment and not only to talk about it. I believe that Bowlby's ability to communicate this was just as fundamental as his theoretical explanations.

Also, the "family" hospitality at the home of Germana's mother and the meals we had together, with food prepared by us, contributed to making this seminar a human and relational experience, in addition to a scientific one. I was expecting Michela, our first-born daughter, and this gave me a feeling of inner happiness and calm. I shared this experience with Ursula. She, in turn, shared with me memories of her pregnancies and children. It is not easy, she told me, especially for a son, to be confronted with a paternal model of such a high standard. Inside me, a new life had already started, and therefore a new relationship. I believe such closeness with Ursula and John contributed to the harmony of our dyad.

After spending only three days together, the leave-taking of John and Ursula was moving, as of friends of longer standing who hope to meet again. They asked us to go and call on them at their holiday home on the Isle of Skye. When Michela was born, the Bowlbys sent us a gift, together with a well-wishing card, of a scarf made of very soft wool in pastel colours, white, green, and pink. We still keep it, as a tangible symbol of secure attachment.

# A strange guest at our house.
# The encounter with Bowlby in 1985
# viewed in retrospect

*Germana Agnetti and Angelo Barbato*

P ersonal and professional lives are closely intertwined with the acquirement of cultural and scientific knowledge. They are made up of encounters, readings, exchanges, events, and work and study experiences. They are a set of tesserae that periodically are organised into a coherent mosaic. This contribution aims at regarding John Bowlby's seminar in Milan from the point of view of the impact it had on us, and, therefore, at recalling anecdotes and comments on the seminar. Personal experience is not only political, as they used to say in the 1970s, but in our field it is also professional.

In 1984, our friend and colleague, Milly Fumagalli, suggested to Ferruccio Osimo and us that we should invite John Bowlby, whom she had recently met in London, to come to Milan and hold a seminar. We accepted without hesitation. We were impelled by enthusiasm and curiosity, and also by the carefree recklessness that was characteristic of those years.

We were enthusiastic at the idea of organising an event that we felt would be of cultural importance, and curious to get to know such an eminent person as John Bowlby. We were all the more curious because, in the distribution of tasks, we had been entrusted with the logistical operations. The organisation of the seminar was entirely homemade, and our financial resources very limited. Therefore, we asked Germana's mother to put her house at our disposal for two days. It had a very large living room where the seminar could take place, as it actually did. As for Bowlby, since we could not afford to pay for a hotel for him, we offered to put him up at our home. We had a rather large house, with a guest room and garden.

However, we were also rather reckless. It did not occur to us that we were biting off more than we could chew. We were organising an event of great scientific importance—the first clinical seminar to be held in Italy by the father of attachment theory—without money, without institutional and academic backing, and without publicity, except by word of mouth. The Internet was still far in the future. We did not even have a fax machine. We were young people who were esteemed in their circle, but we only had about ten years of professional career behind us and did not occupy any important positions.

However, our recklessness was rewarded. Bowlby accepted, thus showing great broad-mindedness. The seminar was a success and drew about thirty participants, not only from Milan, but also from other cities in North and Central Italy.

What were our interests at the time, and what impact did this meeting, in many ways exceptional, have on our personal develop-

Bowlby and his wife, taken in the garden of Germana and Angelo's house.

ment? We were both MDs and had specialised in psychiatry some years before. Germana had also specialised in psychology, which was then open to MDs. We were both thirty-six years old. We met through professional associations. Our pair relationship was deeply intertwined with the work and interests we shared in the fields of psychiatry and psychotherapy. Some life experiences were different from those of our comrades, others we shared. To begin with, we shared in the renewal of psychiatry that had taken place in Italy in the 1970s and 1980s with the closing of mental hospitals and the development of community psychiatry. In the second place, we wished to integrate political and organisational aspects with a better understanding of our patients' subjectivity. Next, we wished to extend our knowledge, in order not to remain confined within Italian academic psychiatry and the training schools to which we belonged. Finally, we wished to meet people who were making their mark in our field.

We had no prejudice. We were interested in any new approach. In those years, this thirst for knowledge led us to get in touch with Franco Basaglia, Franco Fornari, Gaetano Benedetti, Mara Palazzoli Selvini, David Cooper, Johannes Cremerius, Félix Guattari, Solomon Resnik, Hanna Segal, Loren Mosher, Salvador Minuchin, and Robert Castel, and also with others whose names are now forgotten, or with people of dubious reputation, such as Maharish Maresh Yogi and Jacqui Lee Schiff.

We were interested not only in people, but also in places. We travelled a lot and tried to take every opportunity to visit real or presumed first-rate centres, which we had learnt about through reading or from seminars. We visited, briefly or more at length, the Mental Hospital of Trieste, the Tavistock Clinic, the Arbours Association communities, the Mental Research Institute, Soteria House, the Langley Porter Neuropsychiatric Institute, and even Esalen and the Institute of Transpersonal Psychology in California.

Impelled by this thirst for knowledge, we could not lose the opportunity of a training experience with Bowlby. It was new to us, because we were not well acquainted with attachment theory. Germana had studied it summarily in her psychology course, and Angelo had only some general knowledge of it. In our psychiatric training in Milan, Bowlby was never mentioned, and none of the textbooks of psychiatry then in use mentioned attachment theory in its index.

Even if the teaching of psychiatry in Italy in those years had a limited scope, it is surprising that two well-educated and attentive psychiatrists should have had such limited knowledge of attachment theory and its developments, considering that Bowlby's first contributions had appeared nearly forty years before.

In order to understand this, we must go back to the situation then prevailing. After the war, official psychiatry in Italy was asphyxial. Psychology had been fully introduced only recently into our country. Many developments in psychotherapy reached the Italian public very late. *The Psychoanalysis of Children*, by Melanie Klein (1960), first published in 1932, was only translated into Italian by a small publishing firm in 1969; the 1951 book by Ruesch and Bateson, *Communication: The Social Matrix of Psychiatry*, appeared in 1976; Jacques Lacan's *De la psychose paranoïaque dans ses rapports avec la personnalité* (1932), was first published in Italy only in 1980.

This, however, is only part of the explanation, because Bowlby's trilogy on attachment had already been available in Italy for some years prior to the seminar. There were other reasons. The main one was that Bowlby's work was not particularly attractive for those of us in the mental health field who were immersed in the culture of the 1970s. Starting from the end of the 1960s, there was widespread interest in Italy in psychiatry and psychology, especially in connection with the violation of human rights. These subjects were addressed by political radicals and the anti-authoritarian movement. From then on, there was a boom in enrolments in psychiatry and a growing interest in psychology, which had been recently introduced in universities. Many young doctors who approached psychiatry, and the first group of young psychologists, came from the student movement and wanted to challenge the institutions and practices concerning mental illness. The interest in psychology, family dynamics, psychoanalysis, and structuralism was accompanied by cultural unrest. Those interested in these subjects, coming from medicine, philosophy, or psychology, would participate in seminars and in study, training, and supervision groups, often informal, but very crowded. Even if in the first half of the 1980s things were changing, the influence of the previous decade still held sway. The mental health services were staffed by people of our own age, many of them coming from that sort of experience.

In Milan, there was much interest in psychoanalysis, especially in the Kleinian model. Some young psychiatrists had already trained, or were training, in London. What attracted us was that Klein's thinking offered a key to the understanding of psychosis, which was our main interest. We wanted to fight the dragon at the heart of its fortress, which we were intent on demolishing.

Also, Lacan and his school were concerned with psychosis, in connection with the emphasis laid on the concept of desire. They created a cultural atmosphere that also fascinated many intellectuals interested in mental disorder.

All told, at the end of the 1970s, psychiatry and clinical psychology in Milan oscillated between the French and Lacanian influence, on the one hand, and the British influence linked to Klein and the object-relations school on the other. These interests coexisted with membership of the anti-institutional movement, with no awareness of the inherent contradictions. Franco Basaglia's group, which eventually achieved the closing of mental hospitals, was very wary of psychotherapy, which was considered to be manipulative—a position originally held by Foucault.

Why did Bowlby not benefit from this interest in psychoanalysis? His heretical position should have counted in his favour. This did not happen for two reasons. In the first place, he did not seem to provide instruments for dealing with psychosis. In the second place, he had not created a school and had remained rather isolated, and there was no one engaged in disseminating his ideas. We shall see later on that the first point was due to a hurried and superficial reading of his work.

In the meantime, in Milan, a challenge to the psychoanalytic hegemony came from Mara Palazzoli Selvini's group. Although she had psychoanalytic experience with Benedetti, she then moved away from it and concentrated on the systemic approach, which she applied to family therapy in a highly original manner. This was the first important Italian contribution to psychotherapy. For the first time, it gave rise to a centripetal, rather than a centrifugal, movement. Foreign professionals came to Italy to study, and not *vice versa*. The systemic family approach caught on. It was easier to integrate with social and political commitment than psychoanalysis. It was explicitly meant to deal with severe mental disorders and was more suitable for use in public mental health services. It was compatible with the challenge to the family institution, which was viewed as oppressive, characterised the counter-culture of the 1960s and had been made popular by the writings of Laing and others.

This was the cultural context in which we developed. On the one hand, there were naïveté, errors, contradictions, and oversimplifications. On the other hand, there were ethical considerations, commitment, participation, love of knowledge, and empathy for the suffering of others. They all formed an inextricable mixture.

Our training matched this situation. We had both undergone a Kleinian analysis, which Germana had terminated shortly before the seminar. Our interests were definitely shifting towards the relational approach. Together with her analysis, Germana had trained in systemic family therapy at the school directed by Luigi Boscolo and Gianfranco Cecchin. This sharpened the dilemma between experience and fantasy.

We prepared for the seminar by reading some papers by Bowlby, especially the recent one on "Psychoanalysis as a natural science" (Bowlby, 1981). This event obviously took place at a moment of personal and cultural change. This was emphasised by the fact that Germana was due to leave in August, together with our son, for Canada, where she had obtained a Post-Doctoral Fellowship at the University of Calgary in the family therapy department directed by Karl Tomm. Angelo joined her soon after. Some years later, this sojourn abroad was followed by another in Australia. Both these experiences led to our definitive retreat from psychoanalytic models.

The search for conceptual tools was becoming more systematic and the de-institutionalisation of those with mental disorders was being concluded. A new approach was called for. Those who had taken part in the renewal of psychiatry started taking an interest in evaluative research. This led Angelo to take part in a course in psychiatric epidemiology held by Viviane Kovess in Paris.

Most of the participants in the seminar had a classical or Kleinian psychoanalytic background. However, even those without a strictly Kleinian training were aware of the thinking of Klein and her followers and were attracted by it.

After more than twenty-five years, we have lost track of most of the participants and have only vague recollections of them. With others, we have kept in touch, or we had the opportunity of contacting them again before writing this report, as one does with old schoolmates. Certainly, the fact of having personally met Bowlby had a special impact on us. We heard him speak of his personal contrast with Klein, notwithstanding his own Kleinian analysis with Joan

Riviere, and of the claustrophobic effect of therapy confined within the limits of fantasies and the dyadic relationship without any reference to the context and to what happened in the reality of relationships. All this had an impact far greater than any written text could have had.

After many years, all the participants we contacted retained a clear memory of the seminar. We got the impression that it had introduced a different point of view that continued over time, if only as a safeguard against excessive fascinations. For some, it meant looking at Klein more critically, and, in the long run, it was a stimulus towards critical thinking and intellectual autonomy. Bowlby had transmitted these values through his personal authority. Others were influenced more specifically by this different viewpoint, and it had important consequences for their clinical practice.

For instance, Pelizzaro, an SPI (this is the Italian Freudian association, Società Psicoanalitica Italiana) psychoanalyst, who, together with Osimo and Fumagalli, presented a case, retains a clear memory of those days, and especially of the supervision of her case. The seminar had a great impact on her. It confirmed something she had already glimpsed in her clinical work, which was the importance of real traumas and the need to share suffering. In those days, the statements of orthodox psychoanalysts were mainly transference interpretations, whereas Bowlby's supervision had stressed the importance of the therapist's attitude in determining the patient's reaction.

For all of us, the seminar was an opportunity to confront crucial subjects: real experience, as opposed to fantasy; the importance of recollection, as opposed to construction; dependence, as opposed to attachment. In this connection, Bowlby had emphasised that the concept of dependence is misleading. One should stress attachment. Dependence is a negative construction; it was a real challenge to review the notion of dependence.

The concept of real-life experience highlights the role of the family context and of the wider context in giving rise to mental suffering. Also, the therapist follows this rule. To use Bowlby's terms, the way in which a patient builds up the relationship with the therapist is due not only to the patient's history, but also, to the same degree, to the way in which the therapist treats the patient. Thus, the therapist should be committed to being aware of the nature of her/his contribution to the relationship. Together with other influences, this reflects, in one way or another, what the patient experienced in childhood (Bowlby, 1988).

This highly relational way of thinking of the patient and the therapist–patient relationship concurs with the systemic approach. Notwithstanding the differences in context, it is also connected with the essential tenet of the Italian anti-psychiatric movement: the impact of treatment on the patient.

The seminar could, thus, be the starting point for reflections on the compatibility of various types of therapeutic operations within a coherent framework. There was something important linking the anti-psychiatric movement, attachment theory, and the systemic family approach. Maybe, at that time, we were prey to a sort of intellectual bulimia that made us shift from Laing to Lacan, to Klein, and, why not?, also to Bowlby, without thinking about what linked these authors and what separated them. It did not matter what the theoretical framework of the various contributions was, provided they somehow nourished our minds and gave us tools with which to operate. We applied the dictum of Deng Xiaoping: "It does not matter whether the cat is white or black, provided it catches the mice".

Today, nearly thirty years later, we realise the risks connected with this approach. It could lead to fragmentary operations and to not attaining a coherent narrative that takes into account the multiple levels involved in mental suffering.

Memories of the seminar are intertwined for us with those of the conversations we had with Bowlby and his wife, Ursula, when they were guests at our home. Although we had prepared their stay with great care, we had not thought of certain important details that maybe did not make our house completely comfortable for guests such as they. To begin with, they had to go up a spiral staircase to reach their room, which was not easy for people their age (Bowlby was then seventy-eight years old). In the second place, their room was separated from the corridor leading to our own room and that of our five-year-old boy not by a door, but only by a curtain.

Notwithstanding these drawbacks, the prevailing atmosphere was warm and unconventional. At the start we were very worried. Bowlby had the appearance and attire of an English gentleman of bygone days, seemingly far removed from our own very informal manners. This impression quickly dissipated. The two of them behaved in a simple and modest way. They were courteous but friendly, without taking on a parental attitude, which could have been justified by the difference in age. Actually, Angelo was born the same year as their last-born son Robert, and Germana was born the year after.

Our conversation mixed personal and professional subjects, and our guests behaved as if they had known us for a long time. The most extraordinary thing was the naturalness of it all. They both told us much about their past, their family, and the conflicts and difficulties encountered in the psychoanalytic environment. They spoke of their great pleasure in being grandparents. Bowlby thought he was much better as a grandfather than he had been as a father, because work had not allowed him to devote much time to his children. He regretted that none of his children had followed in their father's footsteps, but he had hopes that one of his grandchildren would do so. We spoke of the preparations for our departure for Canada. We also spoke about infantile autism. Bowlby thought it is due to genetically determined constitutional factors, which could be partially influenced by the type of attachment, either positively or negatively. He related anecdotes concerning the tumultuous period during the war, when the British Psychoanalytical Society was torn between the followers of Anna

From left to right: John Bowlby, Ferruccio Osimo, his wife, Claudia Ferrandes, Angelo Barbato, Ursula Bowlby, Germana Agnetti with her son, Guido, and crouching in front, Emilia Fumagalli. Taken in the garden of Germana and Angelo's house.

Freud and those of Melanie Klein. Of the latter, he had an unpleasant personal recollection. Among other things, we were struck by a saying of the American philosopher, Santayana, which Bowlby considered emblematic of his approach and which he also cited in the seminar: "Those who cannot remember the past are condemned to repeat it".

Before leaving, Ursula gave us a small English book for our little boy: *The Tale of Tom Kitten*, by Beatrix Potter, in which she wrote a personal dedication. It is still in the bookcase of our bedroom, which is now the one the Bowlbys occupied many years ago.

Time passed, and we did not mention Bowlby any more, but important things remain impressed on the mind, even if we do not realise it, and then re-emerge.

With hindsight, it is clear that at the time we had not perceived the link between attachment theory and the relational approach, which was already evident in Bowlby's first writings. In a paper of 1949, he described how the involvement of the parents had allowed the over-coming of a dead end in the therapy of an adolescent. He added that the consultation with parents had become a common practice in the assessment phase in the department he directed at the Tavistock Clinic (Bowlby, 1949). However, he himself did not follow up on this practice and he never carried out family therapy. He always remained an individual therapist, even with small children.

On the other hand, also in connection with family therapists, attachment theory was ignored for a long time. Notwithstanding the connections that are now obvious, the relational systemic approach to the family and attachment theory remained worlds apart for a long time.

There were some exceptions. Wynne, in an important paper on the epigenesis of relational systems, which appeared in *Family Process* (Wynne, 1984), had suggested a model of family development that took into account four dimensions, among which was attachment–care-giving. In this paper, Wynne repeatedly cited Bowlby. He stressed that Bowlby had observed that attachment behaviour devel-ops in a relational context of recursive feedback. Attachment and care-giving have complementary functions. But, notwithstanding the authority of the author and the journal, there were no significant results. Family therapy remained indifferent to attachment theory and focused almost exclusively on patterns of communication and relational games. The family narrative that was built up in the course of the therapy sessions was practically ignored in respect of the emotional ties that develop in the course of a lifetime within attachment relationships. Adequate consideration was not given to the interpretations of dyadic relationships and their reflection at an individual level.

Ten years had to pass before the importance of attachment theory within the relational approach was recognised. In a paper that also appeared in *Family Process*, Byng-Hall (1995) declared that he wished to make the results of attachment research available also to family therapists. He wrote that attachment lies at the core of family life, that the results of attachment research are highly relevant to family therapy, and that, surprisingly, systemically orientated clinicians had only recently begun to take an adequate interest in it. An opening had been made that led to increasingly important developments.

Almost at the same time, the first textbook describing a clinical model of integration between attachment theory and systemic therapy appeared (Doane & Diamond, 1994). As already indicated by Wynne, the systemic approach was beginning to feel the need to take attachment theory into account.

There are families in crisis whose future is uncertain, who are often unable to explain what happened in the past that led to the present crisis, what is going on in the present, what could lead to a worse situation or, on the contrary, to an improvement in the future. In re-discovering Bowlby, work with these families in crisis was crucial for us. Bowlby and attachment theory had been deposited in our memory. As often happens, this had worked on our professional selves through a slow process of assimilation that is often neither conscious nor explicit.

To begin with, we were aware of having added concern for the emotional aspects of the therapist–patient relationship to our professional tools. We had incorporated the aim, repeatedly stressed by Bowlby, of providing a secure base that allows a critical exploration of one's important relations, even if they are painful ones, without being overwhelmed by them, and of one's past family history. For the rest, we had to await the new century and other opportunities.

Two different events opened our eyes. The first was the increasingly strong evidence of the link between childhood traumas and psychopathology in the adult, even after a long time had elapsed. This had previously been, and partly still is, ignored by many working in the field of psychiatry. It has been confirmed by epidemiological research carried out thanks to generous endowments and sophisticated methods that were not available in Bowlby's day (Varese et al., 2012). Yet, in the seminar, Bowlby himself had spoken of the link between violence endured in childhood and severe mental conditions. We had not paid sufficient attention to this remark. This was the link between Bowlby's ideas and psychosis, to which we did not pay heed.

The second event once more concerns our personal life. It is the exchange of opinions, and the later association, with Gloriana Rangone and Francesco Vadilonga. Through family therapy with adolescents who had undergone trauma and cases of adoption crisis, they arrived at a model that integrates the methods of systemic therapy with the concepts of attachment theory (Bertetti, Chistolini, Rangone, & Vadilonga, 2003; Vadilonga, 2010).

Today, family therapy has assimilated attachment theory, and has in turn enriched it, as often happens in cases of successful integration (Dallos & Vetere, 2009).

We are now convinced that therapy should incorporate a tri-generational family narrative showing influences on dyadic pair and parent–child relations. It is only through this narrative that we can understand the present and try to find feasible alternatives. To question one's way of functioning enables one to ascertain available resources and to find a way out of nightmares that are as extensive as they are incomprehensible.

The systemic therapy developed by the Milan group had a gap that had to be filled by calling attention to models of inner working and emotional ties. All of this could not be ignored, and required an integrative framework both in therapeutic practice and in training.

We need effective tools for use not only by expert therapists, but also by young clinicians. It is difficult to work and teach without making use of such attachment-based methods as the adult attachment interview and the separation anxiety test. They are very useful in exploring dyadic and other significant relationships.

It is important to connect tri-generational relational patterns and family games with attachment relationships with father and mother, and their reflections in internal working models.

To draw conclusions from Bowlby's lesson: real experience prevails over fantasy; internal working models are built on relationships in the present as well as in the past; they might change on condition that there is a shared examination of what happened. We learnt from family therapy that it is necessary to involve, in a flexible way, and according to clinical requirements, the whole family in therapy, especially with children, adolescents, severe emotional and cognitive disorders, behaviour disorders, and addiction. To involve the whole family is a key element that should guide one's therapeutic strategy, even when working with an individual patient.

Maybe Bowlby would agree only partly. Any important training experience leaves seeds that then develop in an autonomous way. We believe this is what happened in those momentous days in 1985.

## References

Bertetti, B., Chistolini, M., Rangone, G., & Vadilonga, F. (2003). *L'adolescenza ferita: un modello di presa in carico delle gravi crisi adolescenziali*. Milan: Franco Angeli.

Bowlby, J. (1949). The study and reduction of group tension in the family. *Human Relations, 2*: 123–128.

Bowlby, J. (1981). Psychoanalysis as a natural science. *International Journal of Psychoanalysis, 8*: 243–256.

Bowlby, J. (1988). *A Secure Base: Parent–Child Attachment and Healthy Human Development*. London: Routledge.

Byng-Hall, J. (1995). Creating a secure family base: some implications of attachment theory for family therapy. *Family Process, 34*: 45–58.

Dallos, R. & Vetere, A. (2009). *Systemic Therapy and Attachment Narratives: Applications in a Range of Clinical Settings*. New York: Routledge.

Doane, J. A., & Diamond, D. (1994). *Affect and Attachment in the Family*. New York: Basic Books.

Klein, M. (1960). *The Psychoanalysis of Children*. New York: Grove Press [Italian translation: *La psicoanalisi dei bambini*. Firenze: Martinelli, 1969].

Lacan, J. (1932). *De la psychose paranoïaque dans ses rapports avec la personnalité*. Paris: Le François [Italian translation: *Della psicosi paranoica nei suoi rapporti con la personalità*. Torino: Einaudi, 1980].

Ruesch, J., & Bateson, G. (1951). *Communication: The Social Matrix of Psychiatry*. New York: Norton [Italian translation: Bologna: Il Mulino, 1976].

Vadilonga, F. (Ed.) (2010). *Curare l'adozione. Modelli di sostegno e presa in carico della crisi adottiva*. Milan: Cortina.

Varese, F., Smeets, F., Drukker, M., Lieverse, R., Lataster, T., Viechtbauer, W., Read, J., Van Os, J., & Bentall, R. P. (2012). Childhood adversities increase the risk of psychosis: A meta-analysis of patient-control, prospective and cross-sectional cohort studies. *Schizophrenia Bulletin, 38*: 661–671.

Wynne, L. (1984). The epigenesis of relational systems: a model for understanding family development. *Family Process, 23*: 297–318.

# Experiential–dynamic psychotherapy: a therapeutic application of attachment theory

*Ferruccio Osimo*

## Introduction

O ver the past three decades, the scientific soundness of Bowlby's research has become irrefutable by psychologists and psychotherapists. Different theoretical models, however, differ as to how to combine the findings of attachment theory with pre-existing theory and clinical practice. The vantage point of experiential dynamic therapies (EDT) in this regard can be encompassed within two main points: (1) their birth and development date back to the 1970s–1980s, making them contemporary to the birth and development of attachment theory. As a consequence, from the beginning, EDT therapists could regard attachment trauma as the major source of human emotional suffering and psychopathology; (2) the systematic video recording of therapeutic sessions led to the displacement of some of the attention from the theoretical framework to the actual therapeutic relationship, making it possible to directly observe and closely regulate the therapeutic operation, reducing the distance between theory and clinical practice, and introducing a higher level of fine-tuning.

Here, the paradigm and setting of EDT is introduced, and the relevant literature on its links with attachment theory is reviewed. The ways in which intensive experiential–dynamic psychotherapy (Osimo, 2003; Osimo & Stein, 2012) can heal pathological attachment is first theoretically discussed and then exemplified with a case study, with a fourteen-month follow-up.

## The experiential–dynamic paradigm and setting

Experiential–dynamic therapies descend from the line of thinking and research historically initiated by Alexander and French (1946), who were the first to declare their aim of making psychoanalytic therapy "briefer and more effective". Before Alexander and French, some of the theoretical contributions by Sandor Ferenczi, Otto Rank, and Wilhelm Reich have been particularly relevant to the development of EDT.

More recently and specifically, Davanloo (1990, 1995) is the most prominent proponent of intensive short-term dynamic psychotherapy (ISTDP), the father of all subsequent experiential dynamic models. Malan recognised the high relevance of Davanloo's contribution to psychotherapy in general, and lent his sophisticated knowledge of psychodynamics to generate a theoretical framework for Davanloo's work. ISTDP has two main distinctive technical features: (i) a new conceptualisation of defence mechanisms and a new strategy in dealing with the way they are met in the here-and-now of the session; (ii) the techniques leading to rapid uncovering and experiencing of even the most primitive layers of human feeling and impulse, shedding light on aspects of human conflict—indeed, of human nature—that would not often surface in the short-term, if not unlocked by way of highly specific techniques. ISTDP is especially suitable for highly resistant personality disorders presenting with ingrained character pathology. To break through these character defences, Davanloo recommends a standard set of interventions, the "central dynamic sequence" (Davanloo, 1989, pp. 35–36), which incorporates the major technical interventions in the process of unlocking unconscious emotion. At the core of this sequence is pressure for feeling. Resistance is, thus, mobilised in the form of tactical and character defences. As defences come to the fore, they can be clarified and challenged by the therapist. This promotes deeper and deeper emotional experiencing, until new defences are mobilised and come to the fore. These new defences are clarified and challenged in their turn, and the process continues in this way until a breakthrough of feeling occurs, followed by an unlocking of the unconscious, that is, when the therapist and patient have a clear view of the pathological components within the psyche. After this has happened repeatedly, the unconscious becomes open and fluid. According to Davanloo, this means that there is no resistance in operation and the deep dynamic content can now flow freely.

Over the past three decades, we have witnessed the birth and development of experiential–dynamic therapies (EDT). EDT originates from the work of Davanloo and that of Malan (1963, 1976a,b, 1979, 1986a,b). It is an evolution of brief psychotherapy, enabling the facing of complex clinical problems and the achievement of a satisfactory change in a relatively short time. A customary feature of EDT is that clinical work is video-recorded, enabling us to view real therapy sessions and provide accurate annotated transcripts. Witnessing audio-visual recordings of real therapies can have a strong impact, especially when it includes intense emotional experiencing as well as the opportunity to directly observe character change. Video technology also gives us an opportunity to play back the process of change and its outcome in a vivid and real way. Davanloo was the first to apply video technology to psychotherapy on a large scale for his research studies and scientific presentations, which proved stimulating to many. His former trainees identify with his psychotherapeutic method to a greater or lesser extent, each emphasising certain aspects and introducing new ones, or even creating new approaches, attuned to, and enriched by, their own personalities. Generally, these EDT approaches are more powerful than previous forms of short-term intervention, since they can be effective in a relatively short time for people presenting with complex problems, severe symptoms, and a strong resistance to change. In the EDT setting, therapist and patient sit in front of each other, preferably without anything, such as a table, between them. It is customary to audio- and video-record therapeutic sessions so as to enable both therapist and patient to review sessions whenever they find it appropriate or useful. Patient and therapist generally review sessions independently and, in most cases, this does not take place after each session. Recorded sessions can be used also for study and teaching purposes if a patient has agreed to this in writing. More generally, no recording can take place before a patient has been fully informed and has signed a consent form. If the patient does not give consent, the therapy can still take place without recording if the therapist agrees to this. Sessions are generally scheduled once a week and have fifty to sixty minutes' duration. Some therapists find it useful to have longer sessions, such as ninety minutes each fortnight. The initial one or two interviews are always longer, lasting two and a half to three hours each. EDT especially aims to bring about activation and experiencing of emotion, and this needs time. This is the reason that therapists, especially at the start of therapy, might allow more time. This initial part of EDT is called the "trial therapy" (Davanloo, 1986), or "trial relationship" (Osimo, 2001), because its main purpose is to assess how a patient responds to exposure to EDT therapeutic techniques, as well as to the relationship with the therapist.

Over the past three decades, various EDT approaches originating from Malan's and Davanloo's pioneering work have been empirically tested and scientifically investigated. Each of them has some characteristic features of its own, whereas other features are common to all. Some of Davanloo's former students went on elaborating Davanloo's theoretical–technical framework, keeping the founder's acronym (e.g., Abbass, 2002; Coughlin Della Selva, 1996; ten Have-de Labije, 2001a,b, 2010), or modifying it slightly, as in attachment-based (AB-)ISTDP (Neborsky, 2003). Others modified some of Davanloo's theoretical–technical principles and the new acronyms are indicative of differences rather than similarities. Examples include accelerated empathic therapy (AET) (Alpert, 1992; Fosha, 1992; Sklar, 1992), accelerated experiential–dynamic psychotherapy (AEDP) (Fosha, 2000, 2003; Russell & Fosha, 2008), intensive experiential–dynamic psychotherapy (IE-DP) (Osimo, 2002, 2003; Osimo & Stein, 2012), mindfulness-informed experiential–dynamic therapy (MI-)EDT (Kalpin, 2003, 2008), personality-guided relational psychotherapy (Magnavita, 2005), and short-term anxiety-regulating therapy (START), also known as affect phobia therapy (McCullough Vaillant, 1997; McCullough et al., 2003). McCullough, though, never abandoned the STDP acronym.

## Intersections of experiential–dynamic models and attachment theory

Four experiential–dynamic authors are considered, whose work is especially informed by attachment theory: Fosha, McCullough, Neborsky, and the present author.

Fosha (2009) describes three factors by which AEDP (see above) can heal pathological attachment patterns. To illustrate the first factor, *surprising the unconscious*, she mentions

> Mary Main, speaking about the efficacy of the AAI, the Adult Attachment Interview, one of the most robust research tools ever developed, as being based in 'surprising the unconscious' (Main & Goldwyn, 1998). One way to get a lot of therapeutic traction is to surprise the patient's unconscious, conditioned as it is by past experience. Their resources overwhelmed, patients come into therapy prepared to have the worst in themselves exposed. To be met not only with compassion and empathy, but also delight and appreciation of one's strengths and qualities, is the last thing that a patient—down and out, feeling scared, overwhelmed, and defeated—expects. To do so is disarming and rapidly undoes defences, yielding access to more viscerally felt, right-brain-mediated emotional experiences, which, in my work, constitutes the stuff of therapy. (pp. 44–46)

According to Fosha, the second factor is, *undo the patient's aloneness in the face of intense emotional experience*, since experiencing oneself as alone is the cost paid by the child as a consequence of "defensive exclusion" (Bowlby, 1980). She recommends,

> Clinically, in order to render defence mechanisms no longer necessary, and to gain access to the emotions that have gone offline, it is crucial to undo the patient's unwilled and unwanted aloneness. With traumatizing experiences, *being with* is necessary but not sufficient. When it comes to the regulation and processing of heretofore feared to be unbearable emotions, active engagement, that is, sleeves rolled up feeling and dealing right along with the patient is what is required. (p. 47)

This "has to do with the judicious, mindful use of the therapist's own affect". Fosha's third factor is the *child's sense of existing in the heart and mind of the other* (Fosha, 2000, p. 57, italics added). Interestingly, Fosha highlights that it is crucial to

> explore the patient's *receptive* affective experiences of the therapist's presence, care, compassion, and love, i.e., what it feels like to *feel* understood, cared for or delighted in. Crossing that receptive barrier

> ... requires that you (a) explicitly express how the patient exists in your heart and mind, and (b) actively explore the patient's experience of you, all the more so when the experience is positive. ... A simple way of doing this is through raising the question 'what is your experience of me?' and then experientially exploring that experience with the same interest, curiosity and rigor as any other emotionally laden experience. (p. 57)

McCullough's (McCullough Vaillant 1997; McCullough et al., 2003) affect phobia therapy is a most remarkable example of a therapeutic model specifically and explicitly moulded on research findings. The emphasis it places on the freeing of emotion and the techniques it provides to pave the way to emotional experiencing are, by themselves, an antidote to defensive exclusion. McCullough substantially endorses Tomkins' (1962, 1963) theory of affect, according to which there are three motivational systems at the root of specific action tendencies: biological drives, physical pain, and affects. "As Tomkins pointed out, *affects are the primary motivator of behavior*, because affects amplify or intensify whatever experience they are associated with" (McCullough et al., 2003, p. 15, original emphasis). And, "*If affect is the fundamental motivational force in human nature, then affect needs to be central in our clinical theory and practice, in order to have a strong impact on changing patients' behavior*" (McCullough et al., original emphasis). The importance of attachment behaviour is constantly emphasised by McCullough, who regards attachment theory also as an evolution of the Freudian concept of *repetition compulsion*. In her words,

> There are many people who repeatedly choose unhealthy, destructive or injurious relationships. In psychodynamic terminology, this phenomenon has been viewed as an example of the repetition compulsion—a term that refers to the symptom, not the aetiology. It can also be looked at as *addictive attachment*, in which addiction is understood as continued use despite negative consequences. (McCullough et al., 2003, p. 279, original emphasis).

She (McCullough et al., 2003, p. 18) effectively summarises her theoretical position as follows:

> Although cognition (thought) has generally received more attention than the experience of affect, this model of STDP focuses on affect, for

these reasons: affect is the primary system for motivation and there-fore for change. Affective connections that have been learned can be unlearned and relearned. Affect is not always conscious, and thus can be easy to miss. Affect can be difficult to face and bear, and thus is easily sidestepped if it is not addressed systematically. Affect emerged before cognition in the process of evolution, and is processed sepa-rately and often before cognition in the brain. Affect emerges before cognition in the development of the infant. Focus on affect has demon-strated effectiveness in two clinical trials of STDP (Winston et al., 1991, 1994; Svartberg et al., 2004) and in a number of process studies, reviewed in McCullough, 1998, 2000.

Fosha, McCullough, and Neborsky are all former disciples of Davanloo. As we notice, Fosha, McCullough, Neborsky, and the present author gave birth to new models—AEDP and APT, res-pectively. Neborsky (2003), instead, further developed Davanloo's ISTDP, putting a specific emphasis on the impact of early trauma on adult character problems. His "attachment-based ISTDP", explicitly bases the treatment of mental disturbances (American Psychiatric Association, 2013) on attachment theory. A recent clinical study (Neborsky & Bundy, 2013) matches the adult attachment interview (AAI) to observation of a video-recorded, ISTDP single interview of 2–3 hours duration, measuring the concordance between the two in accurately determining a subject's attachment pattern. Interviewers were blind to the results of the AAI, which were scored and classified independently. They used the adult attachment clinical rating scale (AA-CRS), which is an adapted version of the AAI "states of mind scales", in conjunction with the structured ISTDP interview, in order to obtain the main classifications and sub-classifications. By categoris-ing each patient's defences, pathways of anxiety discharge, and qual-ity of an observing and attentive ego, and discussing the clinician's knowledge of the patient's attachment history, the interviewers predicted seven out of eight AAI main classifications correctly, and five out of eight AAI sub-classifications correctly, indicating that there was a statistically significant relationship between predicted and expected values for main classifications and sub-classifications. Even considering that the sample was of eight patients only, this study shows that a comprehensive single clinical interview, if informed by attachment theory, can provide an accurate evaluation of a patient's attachment pattern.

## *Intensive experiential–dynamic psychotherapy (IE-DP)*

Intensive experiential–dynamic psychotherapy (Osimo, 2002, 2003; Osimo & Stein, 2012) is a therapeutic model mainly originating from Malan's (1976a,b, 1979) brief psychotherapy, and Davanloo's ISTDP (1990, 1995). A prominent characteristic of IE-DP is that it strives to balance and harmonise the use of techniques with the *real* relationship with the patient. This implies that taking care of the real relationship is regarded to be *as important as* technical intervention. What is meant here by "real relationship" is the most personal part of the interchange, which is all that is common to human relationships, therapeutic or otherwise. The encounter of two people creates a unique interpersonal current, flowing in largely unconscious and mysterious ways. This is regarded as a fundamental ingredient of both the actual relationship and the transformational process. Tuning into and giving attention to these very personal aspects of the therapist–patient relationship can significantly empower any technical intervention. Putting a premium on human connection and closeness creates the potential for patients to benefit from feeling the therapist's genuine interest in them, and perceiving the therapist as a *true person*. This makes the therapeutic action more powerful. In IE-DP, the patient's whole person—rather than his or her pathology—is the focus. As a therapeutic approach, IE-DP highlights three key characteristics: (i) the real relationship between patient and therapist, (ii) emotional experience in body and mind, and (iii) technical interventions. The IE-DP therapist takes a comprehensive view of the patient–therapist relationship that is seen as both a real, personal interchange between human beings and a matrix enhancing the healing power of all technical interventions. This involves a total openness on the therapist's part. Physical (through the body) and mental (related mental representations, thoughts, and fantasies) experience of feelings, impulses, and desires are actively facilitated, and valued as deep and meaningful expressions of the Self. Technical interventions include identifying unhealthy defences and motivating their renunciation, regulating anxiety to ease distress, and facilitating emotional experiencing of deep feeling and impulse. In addition, the therapist aims at identifying the overall character hologram (Osimo, 2009; Osimo & Stein, 2012) and the self-sabotaging aspects of character and superego. IE-DP retains the term "superego", drawn from Freud (1923b, 1924c), redefined as a set of inner guidelines and psychological functions influencing the individual's life strategy, which starts developing from the very early phases of life, results from the interplay and interaction of the individual with the physical, relational, and cultural environment, and is largely unconscious (Osimo & Stein, 2012, p. 100). This definition of superego is closer than the Freudian one to Bowlby's (1982, pp. 80–83) concept of "inner working model". The therapist also calls upon all the individual's resources to establish the supremacy of the Self. Interventions also clarify links between the patient's in-session experience and behaviour with the therapist and those with significant others in their current life and past, to make dynamic sense of conflicting emotion and recurrent maladaptive patterns. Individuals are helped to make relationships with an Other and with the Self more adaptive, with regard to both the handling of actual relationships in life and their inner representation. Application of therapeutic interventions is guided by close monitoring of the moment-by-moment shifts of the patient around the corners of the "triangle of conflict" (Figure 1), rather than a predetermined sequence of therapist activities.

In other words, a therapist's choice of intervention is guided by the way the therapeutic relationship unfolds, as well as by careful assessment of what is at the forefront, that is, impulse/feeling, anxiety, or defence, using the "triangle of experiential–dynamic activities" (Figure 2) (Osimo, 2001) as a compass.

These endeavours pave the way to the powerfully healing in-session experience of deep, painful feeling and impulse in an

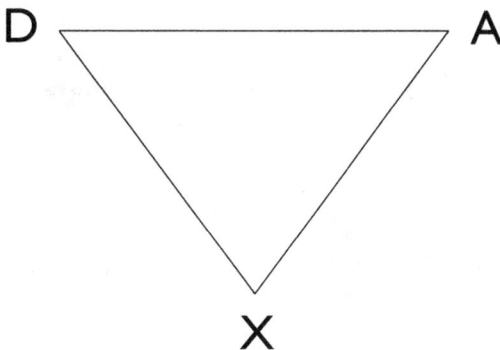

*Figure 1.*    Triangle of conflict.

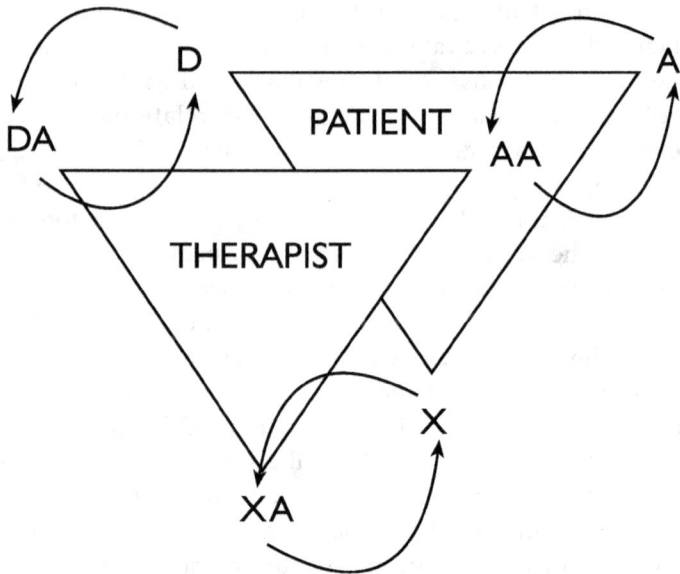

*Figure 2.*    Triangle of experiential–dynamic activities.

atmosphere of safety and interpersonal connection, enabling the individual to promote the desirable changes in a reasonably short time.

In a recent book (Osimo & Stein, 2012) a coding system based on nine therapist activities was developed to assist the reader in making sense of the clinical dialogue. The nine activities considered are: taking care of the real relationship (RE), active mirroring (MI), history taking, perspective, and portrayal (HP), as well as high technical content interventions, that is, defence restructuring (DA), emotional maieutics (XA), anxiety regulation (AA), dealing with the superego (SE), making dynamic links (TCP), and restructuring representations of self and others (SO).

## Consistency of IE-DP and attachment theory

Having introduced IE-DP, we can now highlight four points that make it consistent with attachment theory. This is later illustrated with a clinical example.

*Therapist's attitude toward real-life events*

I start from a personal anecdote. In the early 1980s, during my train-ing in psychotherapy at the Tavistock Clinic, the consulting room I shared with a fellow trainee was on the same floor, the fourth, as John Bowlby's. As customarily happens in the psychoanalytic milieu (prob-ably due to an ethological law), one's own specific interest area absorbed everyone. For example, group analysts were enthusiastic about Bion, and felt empowered by the power of groups, Kleinians were sated by exploiting the bad breast–good breast and throwing projections of split parts, and I was totally focused on focal psycho-therapy and the follow-up study I was carrying out under Malan's guidance (Malan & Osimo, 1992). As a result of this, and notwith-standing the proximity of our rooms, I managed to complete my psychotherapy training ignoring—and remaining untouched by—Bowlby's work.

Curiously, my exposure to attachment theory was initiated on my return to Milan, and is to the credit of Marco Bacciagaluppi (1985, 1989a,b, 1994, 2012), one of the first to recognise the universal value of attachment theory. When we invited Bowlby to give a workshop in Milan, I had many chances to talk to him directly, and I remember asking what I felt to be a challenging question: "John, your claim is the only thing that matters is real-life events: do you believe that the content of psychotic delusions is also reflecting real-life events?" To my dismay, his answer was affirmative, and the impact it had on me lives on to this day. This anecdote shows the strong impact these two life events—encountering Marco and John respectively—had on my personal and professional evolution. This was actually the reason that, when I subsequently trained in ISTDP with Davanloo in Geneva (1988–1991), I felt that the quasi-surgical emphasis he put on the power of techniques was to the detriment of the real parts of the ther-apist–patient relationship. As a consequence, I developed IE-DP as a real relationship-based therapeutic model. Every theoretical model is built around a few basic assumptions, which make it especially fit to address given types of psycho-emotional problems. The main basic assumption of IE-DP is that the real therapist–patient relationship has the lion's share in determining treatment effectiveness. An assump-tion, by definition, does not need to be proved. However, as Mac-Donald (Osimo & Stein, 2012, p. 411) reminds us, "Over thirty years of meta-analyses and comparative trials have pointed to equivalent outcomes for different models of therapy (Lambert & Ogles, 2004; Wampold, 2001)". So, a possible explanation of this observation is that the real relationship is the "third variable", which weighs more than the therapeutic model employed. This view of things is highly consistent with attachment theory, since a real relationship-based model such as IE-DP aims to expose the patient—even in the short term—to a good enough, hence healing, attachment experience in the relationship with the therapist. It is not by chance that the major emphasis of IE-DP training is on how to blend an active care of the real relationship with the use of techniques. We can conclude that "taking care of the real relationship" is as central to IE-DP as "real-life events" are to attachment theory. This is consistent with Bacciagaluppi's (2012, p. 55) statements, "Attachment theory might provide a new metapsychology for psychoanalysis, based on evolutionary theory"; and,

> Attachment theory places psychoanalysis on a firm evolutionary basis and links it to the extensive research on child development that has been generated by the theory. The psychoanalytic method is retained and attachment theory is adopted as an alternative paradigm.

### Attachment pattern, character hologram, and self-sabotage

Referring to the child's attachment pattern and the mother's complementary care-giving behaviour, Bowlby (1988, p. 80) writes, "A person's whole emotional life . . . is determined by the state of these long-term, committed relationships". This statement clearly implies the choice of focusing on the relational interaction, rather than dealing with the individual as an isolated entity. At the same time, this way of considering "a person's *whole* emotional life" seems related to the concept of character armour developed by Reich (1945) and to the therapeutic use of the character hologram (Osimo, 2009; Osimo & Stein, 2012, pp. 107–132), both of which are ways of addressing the character in its *wholeness*.

> The idea of a *character* hologram is to produce a three-dimensional image of the character that is perceived by the patient in a bright and vivid way. Patients are more often aware of one aspect of their character but not another. For this reason, the character image needs to be *whole* as, otherwise, patients might go on seeing only those character

aspects of which they are already aware but not, to put it this way, the other side of the moon. (Osimo & Stein, 2012, p.109, my italics)

As the case study will illustrate clinically, the character hologram is an intervention designed to make the individual's character—at the root of which lies his or her pattern of attachment—visible to the patient. The effect of directly addressing the pattern of attachment in this way is to de-repress the emotional experience of the feelings that the patient hitherto defended against, countering—in Bowlby's terms—the defensive exclusion. The exclusion of feelings, thoughts, and memories originating from early trauma and maintained by the attachment pattern is in this way undone, and the self-depriving and self-sabotaging vicious circle starts cracking.

## Parallel observations

Attachment theory was largely made possible by experimental settings designed to directly study the complementary attachment behaviours in child and care-giver. In a similar way, Davanloo's ISTDP and the experiential–dynamic therapeutic models resulting from it owe their existence to empirical research based on a systematic use of video-recording of therapeutic sessions. So, interestingly, both paradigms have developed around multiple and accumulated evidence from observable phenomena. However, attachment research has focused on the discovery and identification of the forces governing human attachment. Experiential–dynamic models have, instead, privileged the therapeutic side, and placed the identification and healing of self-sabotaging attachment patterns at the core of therapeutic operation.

## Corollaries and recapitulation

1. IE-DP places emotional experience at the centre of the therapeutic process. Enabling the person to access his/her emotional life, that is to be oneself, is in itself an antidote to defensive exclusion.
2. IE-DP actively fosters the creation of a good enough real relationship with the therapist. This gives the patient a relational experience that can correct her/his perception of the relationship

with the other (Osimo, 2003, pp. 4–10; Osimo & Stein, 2012; pp. 44–49), hence, their pattern of attachment.

3.    IE-DP has a radical position regarding the priority of real-life events and the real relationship with the therapist.

4.    IE-DP can be regarded as a way of applying attachment theory to clinical practice, and provides a further confirmation of the centrality of attachment in human life.


## Case study

This therapy was carried out in Italian, and I translated the following excerpts into English.

The patient presented with a depressive breakdown, seemingly precipitated by the threat of her relationship with her boyfriend coming to an end. During the first extended interview, it was possible to create a good enough real relationship with the patient, assess symptoms accurately, explore and regulate anxiety (which turned out to be discharged via the striated musculature without any somatisation or interference with cognition and perception), start dealing with the superego, get to the emotional experience of rage at mother, and bring into focus the character hologram of the "little ill one".

Here is an outline of the case.

*Symptoms*: regression: went back to stay with parents, spending her time in bed; lost her usual self-confidence and initiative; depressive inner feelings.

*Character*: being abandoned by the first boyfriend with whom she felt deeply involved, surfaced problems with emotional closeness; she was always superficially sociable, but avoidant of real involvement. As the character hologram will bring to the open, she is dependent, plaintive, and tends to regress to the mode of "the little ill one".

*Therapeutic strategy*: by bringing to the open character defences and superego aspects, it was possible to achieve character change and restructure the self–other relationship.

*Excerpts*:

- First extended session: character hologram.
- Session 2: handling of regressive and passive aggressive defences.

- Session 8: real relationship, a healing ingredient.
- Session 19: end of therapy.
- 14-month follow-up: therapeutic outcome.

## Excerpts from the first extended interview

As is customary in IE-DP, the first interview can be extended to up to three hours. During the first twenty minutes of the interview, the patient talked about her life, symptoms, and complaints, keeping a rather superficial, uninvolved attitude. The therapist has attentively listened to her account, asking for clarifications, and observing her overall attitude and non-verbal communications. The intervention that follows is the presentation of the character hologram (Osimo, 2009; Osimo & Stein, 2012). It aims at making visible the overall position taken by the patient. This is likely to shed light also on a few facets of this overall position that are unknown—and, therefore, new—to the patient. This, in turn, is likely to mobilise the patient's anxiety as well as her deep emotion. In the following dialogue, the first italicised text highlights the pattern of attachment used by the patient, the second italicised text the defensive exclusion.

> *Therapist (T):*   In a way you cannot but be that way . . . it's as if there were two faces: one, as you say, is more external, like a façade, of a young woman who is strong, resourceful, capable, full of initiative . . . even being a kind of driving force . . . and this part of you works well, it is a skill you have . . . it seems, however, that this part covers up another part of you, that we perhaps don't know, but there are some clues we have . . . one is that since January, for a number of months, in the relationship with Steve you became like a kid—as you described it—*a kid that is clinging in an angry way: you must not leave me . . .. don't you dare go away* . . . and, also, as you were speaking, I don't know if you noticed, here with me, especially at certain times—I didn't want to interrupt you too often—your voice almost cracked . . . and, even, repeatedly, you made some reference to something you miss . . . something you don't exactly know what, but you need to retrieve it . . . and even this symbolic "going backwards" to take up university again . . . I believe there is more to it than your love of studying . . . It's as if you were looking for something you cannot find . . . a part of you that has a very clear and intense feeling of what you are, want, and feel . . . *and you seem to make an effort to keep at bay this part of yourself* . . . also because whenever it comes back, it gives you hell, turning you into a clinging,

angry, and powerless child . . . so, we'd better go and see this part of the clinging, angry, and powerless child . . . what do you think?

*Patient (P):*   Well, yes . . . yes, yes . . . (smiles).

While presenting the character hologram, the therapist gives attention to the non-verbal, noticing both the rise of emotion and the smile covering it up. Hence, the sense of the next piece of dialogue.

T:   You smile, but when I was speaking it didn't occur to you to smile . . .?

P:   No . . . (smiles).

T:   Even now you are smiling . . . can we see, behind this smiling façade, what you feel?

P:   (Sighs)

T:   Because it seems that there is something you feel very intensely, deep inside, if you are not afraid or try not to be . . .

P:   No, it's . . .

T:   . . . tough . . . to present a mask, as you always did . . . you are here and there is no need to smile . . . stay with what you feel . . . you don't need to find the words at once, you may as well breathe . . . to make room for what you feel . . .

The therapist here wishes to regulate the anxiety ("you may as well breathe"), prevent the patient from resorting to rationalisation, often by gently but firmly interrupting her, and actively to support the emotional experience of her emotion.

P:   I don't manage to . . .

T:   [interrupting] What is it that you are feeling?

P:   No, now, I feel a sort of . . . [sighs]

T:   Take a deep breath . . . let it come . . . [anxiety regulation]

P:   . . . of melancholy . . . I don't know . . .

T:   Let it come . . . let this melancholy come . . . [emotional maieutics]

P:   The point is that then . . .

T:   [interrupting] you reason too much . . .

P:   [smiling, whispering] Perhaps it's true . . .

T:  I do not doubt that you can reason well, but, here, let's look at what you feel . . .

P:  I feel . . . truly . . . exactly as though . . . yes, I believe it is melancholy . . .

T:  Where do you feel this melancholy in your body?

P:  Here [points to a point between her stomach and breast].

T:  There . . . what is it like?

P:  As if I were blue . . .

T:  Something sad?

P:  Yes, as if I were listening to someone who is telling me something sad . . . as if I were given bad news . . . or as if I were watching a sad film and I identify myself with the main character . . .

T:  [pointing out the detachment] So it's as if we were not speaking about you . . .

P:  [sighs] No, because I know we are speaking about me, but it is as though I were looking at some pictures, like flipping through a photo album from . . . something past . . .

The character hologram, plus the therapist's close monitoring of the patient's verbal and non-verbal defensive communication, plus the regulation of anxiety are succeeding in helping the patient get in touch with what she feels. In response, her unconscious is offering a useful clue: a photo from the past, which is an image that probably carries significant and emotionally charged memories. The therapist decides to follow this pathway.

T:  Yes . . . what photo comes to mind?

P:  Well, what comes to mind . . . ["what" is a prelude to generalising, forestalled by the therapist]

T:  What image?

P:  Pictures from when I was a child . . . [the plural, again, is a prelude to generalising]

T:  Do you have a specific one in mind?

P:  Not precisely, no . . . however . . .

T: [observing tension in the striated musculature and in the facial expression] There is a lot of pain in you . . . hmm? . . . let it come . . . don't get stiff . . . you are tense, in your shoulders . . .

P: Yes, I believe I store my tension here . . . I can't see things in a clear way . . . it's as if I saw them out of the corner of my eye . . . anyway, pictures from when I was a kid . . .

T: How old might you have been?

P: Two or three . . . small, not new-born . . .

T: [starts to portray the meaningful incident] Where do you see yourself?

P: On a lawn . . .

T: On a lawn . . . how are you dressed?

P: It is winter . . . with an overcoat . . . with my parents . . . not that I really see them now . . . they are there . . .

T: You know they are there, but you don't actually see them . . .

P: It's as if I were looking through these pictures very fast, but it is exactly that sensation, of when one looks at something past . . . and feels that it is over now, that it will never come back . . .

As is clear in the video-recorded session, the patient's attitude has completely changed. Getting gradually in touch with a feeling of intense sadness has undone her superficially conversational defensive attitude. Having started on a real relationship with the therapist, the process of therapeutic change is now possible. This is a good beginning, but it would be naïve to expect a stable change in the patient's pattern of attachment. The next excerpt, from session 4, aims at illustrating the active handling of another type of defensive detachment, this time in the form of passive aggression.

### Beginning of session 4: passive resistance

The patient arrives at the session in a despondent mood. She presents with a plaintive, passive attitude, and reports that she went back to her parents' home, inviting her boyfriend to join her there.

P: This week didn't go very well . . . hmm . . . it seems to me that I went backwards, especially mood-wise . . . hmm . . . I feel very anxious, though I cannot explain it to myself . . . but . . . I've been pretty low and . . . well, it wasn't much of a week . . . I went back to stay with my parents over the long weekend . . . my boyfriend Steve came over . . . but I feel very passive, that is I don't manage to face things in an active way. I noticed this also at work . . . even though it is not an adverse environment and I am given the freedom to carry out my tasks without a strict deadline . . . I drag things out, I am not proactive, as if I can't get organised . . . as if the day were passing before me and I cannot be active . . . even this past week, there have been a couple of holidays and my friends organised things . . . and I declined their invitation . . . inventing an illness with a temperature . . . because I didn't feel like it, and I try to postpone all that I have to do . . . and that's it . . .

The patient's presentation is clearly a mixture of defensive passivity and feelings that she keeps defensively excluded. The therapist chooses not to empathise with the patient's unhappy predicament. Rather, he wishes to undo the defences of passivity and obstruction. To this end, he addresses the character defence in a way that echoes and carries forward the formulation of the character hologram. This might seem ruthless, but actually aims at overcoming the patient's obstructive position.

T:  You seem to be putting yourself in a very passive position, as you said . . . like an ill person . . .

P:  No, well, I didn't feel like going out and, instead of saying, "no thanks, I am tired", it felt simpler to say I caught a cold and have a touch of flu . . . because if I say, "I don't feel like it", a friend might insist and say, "Come on, it's been a long time since we last met . . .". By saying I am ill with flu, that's it . . .

T:  At any rate you *are* ill, when you take that position . . .

P:  Well . . .

T:  . . . it's an ill-person position you take, even if you are not ill with a cold or flu, but, rather, ill with passivity . . .

P:  Well . . . if you put it that way . . . perhaps . . . I don't know . . .

T:  If you prefer, we can say you take a passive and regressed position, the way you said it . . .

P:  Yes . . . I realised this . . . and . . .

T:  [interrupting to forestall intellectualisation] Then, since it isn't so good to tell friends, "I am passive and regressed", you say, "I have a cold or flu", but . . .

P:  The crux is [the same] . . .

T:  Isn't it?

P:  Perhaps yes . . . and . . .

T:  [interrupting to call attention to her gaze aversion, showing the patient's detachment] And I also noticed that it has been difficult for you to look at me since you arrived here today . . . how is it for you to be here telling me about all this?

P:  Today I didn't feel very much like coming . . . actually, when I feel this way, it is difficult to look at anybody . . .

T:  [interrupting a generalisation and summing up] So, you are passive, regressed, find it difficult to look at me, and didn't feel like coming: this means there is something you feel towards me, because you've "had to" come . . .

P:  Perhaps, as it were, lately my thought . . .

T:  [mirroring and interrupting this speech exercise] Perhaps, as it were, your thought . . . what do you feel?

P:  Embarrassment, perhaps . . .

T:  [in response to this very vague statement, the therapist further mirrors the verbal and non-verbal communication] You are there being passive, even in your (physical) position . . . somewhat bent over on yourself, shoulders down, limp, floppy . . . avoiding my eyes . . . at least before . . . you are finding it difficult to stay connected . . . hmm? . . . and tend to stay passive, folded in on yourself . . . and you say you didn't feel much like coming . . .

P:  Yes, true . . .

T:  So, there is clearly something you feel at the thought of coming and, now, of being here . . .

P:  [sighs]

T:  This sigh, for example . . . shows some anxiety, that means there is something you feel . . .

P:  Well, yes . . . sure . . .

T:  If you don't go limp . . .

P:  I find it difficult . . . this week I find it difficult to do things . . .

T:  [undoing the generalisation] In this moment, you are finding it difficult to be here!

P:  Yes.

T:  So, what do you feel about being here? What is the feeling when you
think about being here?

P:  A bit of unease, even though I don't have any unease at being with
you, however . . . I am annoyed with this situation: I don't feel like
doing this: I feel like lying down, or falling asleep . . .

T:  So, being here and knowing that you'd better be very active and not
passive is annoying you.

P:  Yes, because it takes an effort . . .

T:  Of course it requires an effort! If, with a part of you, you feel like
putting yourself in that passive position and going limp, everything
but falling asleep requires an effort! Doesn't it?

P:  Yes.

T:  So, you are saying you don't feel like being here and having to work
with me.

P:  Hmm . . . I don't feel like it, but not at a rational level, because being
here . . .

T:  [interrupting the rationalisation by calling attention to the body]
Look, you are doubled up . . .

P:  I am always a bit . . .

T:  [challenging the generalisation] Always doubled up?

P:  Yes, I never sit up straight.

T:  So, it's kind of a habit you have, of being bent over on yourself, which
we can see physically, and it is exactly matching your attitude when
you say passive, listless . . . so, this is your method of passive resistance, covering up what you feel about being here and having to be
very active and work with me, hmm? What is it that you feel: I notice
anxiety is beginning, also in your hands . . . [the patient is increasingly
tense in her shoulders and has started fidgeting].

P:  Annoyance, but not because . . .

T:  [interrupting the rationalisation] What do you feel when I wake you
up?

P:   Sure, it makes me realise that . . .

T:   [interrupting the rationalisation] What do you feel?

P:   Annoyance.

T:   So you are annoyed that I disturb your comfort . . . admitting that staying passive and bent is comfortable . . .

P:   Yes, it annoys me, but it makes me angry, because . . .

T:   [interrupting the rationalisation] Where do you feel this anger?

P:   At a physical level?

T:   Yes!

P:   Always in the upper part of my body . . . here and here . . . (pointing to neck and stomach)

T:   Also in your neck? What do you feel in your neck and here [stomach]?

P:   Here, tension, and here like the stomach getting tight . . . and I feel my cheeks have gone red, I don't know if they are . . .

The last two lines show that the patient's wish to work in synergy with the therapist (therapeutic alliance) is starting to prevail on her resistance. The therapist then goes on exploring and actively supporting the patient's feeling part, at the same time mirroring residual defences. This is an example of emotional maieutics (Osimo, 2001, 2003).

T:   Yes, a bit . . . so, if you were to let this anger out, what would you do, or say?

P:   Right now, something really stupid would come . . .

T:   [interrupting to encourage emotional expression, and keep defences at bay] No problem if it appears stupid, provided you don't stay limp and passive, because if you do, nothing will come.

P:   No, it's . . .

T:   Let's see . . .

P:   My first reaction is to say, "Everybody, let me be!"

T:   [undoing the generalisation] To whom?

P:   In general . . .

T:  [undoing the generalisation] There is only me here!

P:  Now it would be with you, but I don't want to . . .

T:  [forestalling the rationalisation and further supporting the emotional expression] Now, here there are the two of us . . . so it's up to you to say, "leave me alone" . . . with that voice, or with a slightly more angry voice?

P:  Perhaps . . . perhaps even with this voice . . .

T:  Plaintive like that?

P:  It is not plaintive, it is annoyed, and . . .

T:  [pointing out the resigned, passive attitude] Yes, annoyed, like someone who is doomed to let others annoy her . . . not like someone who is effective in saying, "Leave me alone!"

P:  Yes, not very decisive. . . .

T:  [role-playing the two poles of the patient's conflict] One part is saying, "Leave me alone!", but the other part says, "Oh, how annoying you are", but conveys that this will have to continue . . . it doesn't really stop the annoying . . . it complains a bit, but takes for granted that I will go on annoying you!

P:  Yes, I take for granted that you will go on, but . . .

T:  [interrupting to avoid rationalisation and support expression]. And that you can't do anything about it . . .

P:  Yes, sure, in a way, I want you to annoy me . . . so there is a split whereby . . .

T:  [forestalling the rationalisation] Let's see, because there is a part that wishes me to come close to you . . .

P:  [interrupting] That is, I . . .

T:  [interrupting] . . . and another part saying, "Oh, how annoying!"

P:  Yes . . . yes . . . yes, yes . . . it's always the same, like when a friend calls me . . .

The patient's spontaneous link is a positive signal. However, the therapist feels that, in order for this type of link to be really convincing and effective, it is safer to give a further boost to emotional experience. Therefore, he again calls attention to the non-verbal. The weepy voice is still screening the emotional experience.

T:  [interrupting] Sorry to interrupt and annoy you a bit more, but . . . do you notice your voice, which is sort of weepy (imitates the patient's voice)?

P:  Yes . . .

T:  I am just imitating the sound . . . so, even your voice reveals this lack of determination, sulkiness, like someone who, at the end of the day, lets others do things even when you don't want . . .

P:  Yes . . .

T:  . . . don't you?

P:  Yes.

T:  What do you feel right now?

P:  Some shame . . .

T:  [interrupting and preventing a possible defensive use of shame] If you look at me and don't withdraw in your little shell . . . there is shame? And about what?

P:  About what you are telling me, because . . . not that I feel told off, but you are goading me about my attitude, that I am showing . . . and somehow you say that it's no good . . . not very productive, etc. . . .

T:  [interrupting to better acknowledge the relevance of the patient's communication] So the shame is about being caught not being productive . . .

P:  Yes, I feel a bit stupid . . .

T:  OK, however, is it you, me, or is it both of us saying it is not so productive?

P:  It would seem it is the two of us, since you made me notice that I should try to, sort of, change my attitude and that I am doubled up . . .

T:  [interrupting and undoing the projection] Did I say you should have a different attitude?

P:  No, no, but . . . you made me notice my being passive, and that my unwillingness to come here meant some non co-operation of mine, like not wanting to work with you . . .

T:  And do you agree on this, or am I wrong in thinking that?

P:  No, I don't actually agree . . . I mean . . . I would prefer not to be here, but I don't even know why, or what else I would wish to do . . .

T:   [interrupting to complete the undoing of projection] I mean, do you agree or not with what you just said, and I said previously, that you are passive and non co-operative?

P:   Generally yes . . .

T:   [undoing the generalisation] And here?

P:   I wish to be co-operative . . .

T:   It's two different things: you might well wish to be co-operative, but do you agree that when you are like this [shows how], you are not being co-operative?

P:   Yes, yes, sure . . .

T:   Because if you don't agree, it's right to tell me . . .

P:   No, no . . . yes, yes . . .

T:   I believe you wish to be co-operative, but, since this is what you wish, we need to look at the ways in which you are not . . .

P:   Sure . . .

T:   . . . or you'll get confused . . . in a way . . . as it actually looks as if you *were* confused, when it comes to staying close *or* staying distant . . . working actively with me *or* instead playing passive and bent over on yourself . . . but this is not with me only, it's also with others . . . and you don't even need to go into details: you said this past week you moved back to stay with your parents—so you went close—and I believe this was out of your choice, was it not?

P:   Yes, yes . . .

T:   OK, so . . . Steve came over—which also means closeness—*but* you were sulky, suffering, passive, regressed, listless . . .

P:   [nods]

T:   So! Staying at your parents' and inviting Steve was your own choice, with a part of you that wanted this . . . or you wouldn't have invited him, or gone to your parents'.

P:   Sure . . .

T:   However [grunts, to convey the patient's attitude]. So, *both parts are there*, you see . . . it's important that we can see it, isn't it? And it happens there as well as here: this is a kind of lab, where we have an experimenting table, represented by this carpet between us . . .

*P:* [smiles]

*T:* And what we see here also happens outside. OK, so, what do you want to do? Stay passive and regressed, or . . .

*P:* No, no, I don't want to stay passive.

*T:* Then, let's see what you wish to do with me here, what you want to face, in what way you can become animated . . .

*P:* [sighs]

*T:* What a sigh!

*P:* [laughs] It's that . . . when you put a question to me like this, the first answer that comes to me is a general answer . . . I don't know what I want to do right now.

If we wish to help the patient to renounce her passive attitude, a declaration of intention is not enough: we need to see if she does take a different attitude.

*T:* . What do you want *to do* to face this passivity of yours?

*P:* I'd like to understand why I keep on . . .

*T:* [undoing the rationalisation] So, you want to understand, not change your attitude?

*P:* No, I want to, but I always think that changing is . . .

*T:* [interrupting] So you want to, but won't . . .

*P:* It's that at times I don't manage . . . that is . . .

*T:* [interrupting to undo passivity and powerlessness] So, now you don't manage?

*P:* Now I do manage . . .

*T:* And what will you do if you change your attitude?

*P:* I will try to take a different attitude, to . . .

*T:* [interrupting to undo tentativeness] Which way?

*P:* More positive . . .

*T:* Let's see!

*P:* I'll try to . . . I don't know . . .

T:   Let's see what you do! If you don't go limp—you see what you do [imitates the patient's posture] . . . for a second you try, then . . . [imitates patient's alternating positions] . . . you see: this is what you do . . . is this the way you want to be in your life?

P:   No, no . . .

T:   When will you start changing? Tomorrow? In a month's time? Or will you start now? [As a consequence of the challenge brought to the patient's defences, her expression shows the surfacing of intensely painful emotion] . . . how come all this pain? What is it, anger? Let's see—if you don't go limp—let's see what it is . . . you have a mouth, and can use it . . .

P:   Well, yes, anger I think . . . perhaps . . .

T:   [interrupting] So, what I said made you angry?

P:   Yes, sure . . .

T:   OK, so you are angry with me because I make you notice you are passive . . .

P:   Yes.

T:   What do you want to tell me to express your anger? If you don't want to stay passive, you will need to bring out this anger . . . what will you do to me?

P:   Absolutely nothing.

T:   What do you want to say?

P:   [shaken, but still withholding some emotion] Well, the first thing that comes to mind is, "It's not true that I am always like this!"

T:   With that small voice?

P:   That is because . . .

T:   [forestalling the rationalisation] Because, because, because . . . it comes because you hold back, you stifle part of your anger, you don't unsheath your claws . . . what would be the way you are if you do show your claws? Let's see the way you are! Unless you want to keep on . . .

P:   No, but I . . .

T:   [interrupting the tentativeness] Let's see what you will do, if you don't want to stay half-paralysed . . .

P:   . . . but one cannot always . . .

*T:*   NOW! Did you come here to get well or to stay ill?

*P:*   However . . .

*T:*   How long do you wish to come here, a year?

*P:*   No . . .

*T:*   Or maybe yes, but . . .

*P.* and *T.* together:   The sooner, the better . . .

The fact of uttering the same words together is an important indicator that, notwithstanding the therapist's aggressive, challenging way of setting about the patient's defences, the therapeutic alliance is strong enough.

*P:*   That's for sure, but, yes it is annoying, but I can't . . .

*T:*   What do you want to tell me?

*P:*   That I am not always like this and you are being too hasty in your conclusions . . .

*T:*   [undoing the patient's projection] Did I say you are always like that?

*P:*   No . . .

*T:*   I said this is the way you are now, is this untrue? Or is it a hasty conclusion?

*P:*   No, it's true, yes . . . and actually . . . yes . . .

*T:*   So what do you want to do, to stay there limp or . . . let out all the strength and the rage you have inside?

*P:*   I don't want to stay limp, but don't know how to express my rage here and now, since I am not angry with you, even if your words annoy me.

By now the quality of the patient's emotional experience is good enough, and the therapist can help the patient link her emotion with a meaningful person/incident in her life, without risking excess intellectualisation and detachment.

*T:*   Here and now, if I didn't put pressure on you, you wouldn't be angry with me: so you are angry with me. It's obvious that, before me, you got angry with others as well in your life, and there is this "being annoyed" that comes over you, as if someone is putting pressure on you and wanting you to do something you don't want to do, and this clearly comes from inside you: you feel they demand of you something you don't want . . . such as making a claim on you or having expectations of some sort . . .

P:  Yes, expectations . . .

T:  Then, let's see what comes to your mind, we don't need to go to China to look for it . . .

P:  I always feel others want something from me: I am afraid I cannot give it, and I find it easier to shoot them: send them away.

T:  Yes, but who in your life expects of you something you cannot give?

P:  To start with, my parents!

T:  Who?

P:  My mum . . ..

T:  Example?

P:  Well, I always felt under pressure, for example at high school, there were years when I was sort of carefree and I didn't bother about school, and I always had this pressure to bring home results . . . she pestered me, "How did it go at school? Did you study? How did the test go?" So I felt my progress at school did not match her expectation . . . so much so that, in my first high school year, she wanted me to move to another school . . . and that I didn't like . . .

T:  Change school . . . for what reason?

P:  [voice breaks, speech is interrupted by violent sobbing] She said I was not capable . . . that perhaps it was too difficult for me.

T:  There is a very violent feeling inside you, at this very moment, hmm?

P:  Hmm, yes . . .

T:  Where do you feel it?

P:  Here . . .

T:  What feeling is it?

P:  Well, some humiliation . . .

We all have been humiliated at least once in our lives, but letting someone humiliate us without fighting them implies taking a passive position. Hence, the next twofold intervention, addressing the defence of passivity and, at the same time, bringing the emotional experience into the here and now.

T:  So, you put yourself in a passive position and let her humiliate you?

P:  The point is that . . .

T:  Or find your voice and say what you wish to say . . . to your mother, in this case . . .

P:  I . . . found it unjust, because . . . school is important, but it's not all . . .

T:  What is the feeling about your mother for this?

P:  I am piss . . . enraged, I find it unjust . . .

T:  How do you wish to tell her, if you don't want to stay passive?

P:  I want to shout it at her!

T:  Shout it! How do you shout it at your mother?

P:  I tell her she doesn't understand anything . . .

T:  [addressing the non-verbal and supporting emotional expression] If you don't bend over on yourself! Do you notice you are doubling up? What do you tell her if you don't bend over on yourself?

P:  That she doesn't understand anything . . . that . . .

T:  You tell her, "You don't understand anything . . ."

P:  Yes, she doesn't understand anything, and . . .

T:  With that voice?

P:   No, well . . .

T:  How do you tell her?!

P   You don't understand anything!

T:  Then? [the therapist wishes to help the patient to fully go through the experience of her emotion]

P:  I tell her she is a shit.

T:  Then what? Do you use the third person?

P:  No, I tell her, "You are a shit", because you never trust me and always stress whatever I do wrong—provided that a low mark in Greek is anything wrong—and, above all, you don't even get angry, but make me feel brain-damaged because I can't do this at school . . .

T:  Hmm, hmm . . . [supporting emotional experience and expression]

P:  . . . in this way you belittle me . . .

T:  Hmm, hmm . . . [supporting emotional experience and expression]

P:  . . . and I don't like this . . .

T:  And this is something that enrages you and also makes you suffer . . .

P:  Well, yes.

T:  . . . that your mother sees you as being below her expectations?

P:  Well, yes . . .

T:  You don't feel she sees you the way you are?

P:  Yes . . .

T:   And that you are not loved for the way you are . . . or not?

P:  Yes, yes!

T:  And this causes you rage and pain?

P:  And makes me sad, yes . . .

T:  So, you play the ill person to get people to cuddle you?

P:  . . . and, actually . . .

T:  To get some kind of compensation? I don't know . . .

P:  Well, yes, certainly it happened, even if she was never very warm . . . neither was she the opposite of this, for God's sake . . . at any rate, I distanced her . . . as if I wanted to punish her . . .

T:  Hmm, hmm!

P:  . . . so, this may be unrelated, but when I was at university, and I was doing very well . . . even when I graduated with honours . . . and I saw she was proud of me, I gave her no satisfaction at all . . . actually her pride, the ceremony, her teary eyes irritated me so much.

T:  What would you have done to her?

P:  I would have slapped her once! [chuckling]

T:  Even twice, since you say you'd slap her and then chuckle . . . to make it softer, perhaps?

P:    Hmm . . .

T:    So, you were really enraged!

This excerpt shows that accurate work on defences can put a patient in touch with intense emotion that was hitherto excluded from consciousness. This type of emotional experience—far from being a purely cathartic exercise—takes place with the patient being fully conscious of the relational, cognitive, and behavioural implications of her feelings. For this reason, it is effective in making possible and promoting the desired change in her character and the related pattern of attachment.

### Session 8: the real relationship with the therapist

As we saw from the previous excerpt, the mother's lack of empathy with the patient's inner self influenced her pattern of attachment. In Session 8, she reports a sensation of not really being listened to, and the therapist decides to focus on the patient's perception of the real relationship with him, challenging her defences against emotional closeness.

P:    To start with, I think the other person does not listen to me . . .

T:    Here, do you feel I listen to you?

P:    Yes, yes . . .

T:    I listen to you?

P:    Maybe you pretend, but my perception is that you listen . . . very much so . . . and I always have a sensation that the other person listens to me out of duty, but in actual fact . . . couldn't care less . . .

T:    [interrupting to undo the generalisation] Here, too?

P:    No, here no. Here I feel important.

T:    Hmm! So I listen to you in what way?

P:    With attention, and also participation . . .

T:    Not out of duty?

P:    No, well, I know you do it out of duty, but . . .

T:    [interrupting to undo the patient's projection] Ah well, since you know . . .

P:   I mean to say . . .

T:   The point is that you don't actually know!

P:   Well, so I imagine . . .

T:   I do this because of my profession, yes. However, this does not say what I feel, does it?

P:   Certainly not.

T:   So, what is your sensation?

P:   That you listen to me . . .

T:   With pleasure?

P:   Yes, well . . . yes . . .

T:   Not out of duty . . . because I feel like it?

P:   [tentatively] Well, yes . . .

T:   Yes or no?

P:   Well, yes! I don't mean to be arrogant!

When confronted with the *reality* of a close, empathic relationship with the therapist, the patient becomes anxious lest she is demanding too much of her therapist/mother. To make this relational experience powerful, it is crucial to actively facilitate the underlying feelings. As it appears, her feelings include being touched by the reality of closeness with the therapist, a warm positive feeling, and sadness about the insufficient closeness she experienced with her primary attachment figures.

T:   Why?

P:   Because it seems like . . . anyway, yes I feel you . . .

T:   You feel?

P:   . . . I feel you are close!

T:   Ah! You *feel* that!

P:   Yes, yes . . .

T:   That's not arrogant; it's what you feel.

P:   Yes, but it might sound somewhat presumptuous . . .

*T:*   It's what you feel, isn't it?

*P:*   Hmm . . . [gradually becoming moved]

*T:*   And is there also an emotion coming?

*P:*   Yes.

*T:*   What emotion is it?

*P:*   That I perhaps . . . am sorry that . . . it feels a bit stupid . . . that is, I am sad that . . . it's that I am moved . . .

*T:*   To start with, let it come! Emotions are good to accept, when they come . . . let them speak.

*P:*   It's like feeling . . . some warmth, in a way . . . and the fact of becoming aware of it, in a way moves me, but I am not sad even so!

*T:*   So there is a nice emotion!

*P:*   Yes, yes . . .

*T:*   Of feeling a warmth . . .

*P:*   Yes, yes . . .

*T:*   . . . in our relationship.

*P:*   [nods, and appears happy and sad at the same time] And, yes, it is a nice thing . . . I am not sad in the least . . .

*T:*   This is nice indeed, we can enjoy it . . . we can take it . . .

*P:*   It is this sense . . . that makes me feel glad to be coming here . . . and it is something I realised in the recent sessions, I must say. It wasn't like this before . . . it is a strange thing, I wouldn't know how to label it, but here I really feel myself!

This vignette shows that the real relationship has the power to undo a person's defensive exclusion of thoughts and feelings originating from real life events, and to heal the painful feelings involved. After another ten sessions, and a final separation from Steve, the patient felt she was well and did not need any further sessions. Parting from the therapist felt a bit difficult, because of the very good relationship that had developed, but it was very warm, too, and the therapist expressed his interest in any news the patient would wish to give about future developments in her life. The therapy had lasted for eighteen sessions, plus the first extended interview.

*Change of character and attachment pattern:*
*fourteen months after termination*

When the therapist called the patient inviting her for a follow-up interview, she was pleased and accepted the invitation. After greetings and saying it was nice to have this chance of seeing each other, they reviewed together the most salient aspects of the patient's inner and external world. A few explanatory comments are in square brackets.

T:  So, in general, how are you?

P:  I am well.

T:  What I am selfishly interested in, is what is better, what worse—hopefully nothing—and what unchanged since your therapy . . . and also if there is anything that specifically makes you believe that therapy was useful.

P:  So: I am certainly more peaceful in general . . . [improved self-regulation of anxiety] . . . a number of times I thought to myself that, before, if I had started on this new job—which was totally new to me and I had to throw myself into it—it would have been absolutely awful! Partly because the work environment is very tough and I and all the others have to go through hell all day long . . . there is always someone dissatisfied, or someone trying to reduce your money . . . [improved self-assertion at work] but I realised that, the moment I am there and I get irritated and think this job is a real pain in the neck . . . cycling home is enough to refresh my head and it's over. In the past, instead, I would have experienced it more personally, you know . . . now, even when I make mistakes, I am much more tolerant . . . I say to myself, "OK, next time I'll be more careful", but I don't have the attitude of: "Shit, what a stupid cow I am, I'm not even capable of doing this!" So I am more relaxed in general, which doesn't mean I don't care, but my attitude is different . . . [change in the inner relationship with self, different attitude to the superego] and . . . something even my friends noticed . . . I became a bit stricter . . . I mean, if there is something I don't like—within the limits of being reasonable, I am not a nuisance—I calmly say so . . . and I don't do it . . . or when they ask for my advice, I am ruthless, and say exactly what I think [improved self-assertion with friends], whereas previously I screened things so as not to hurt others and tried to say what they expected of me . . . and . . . now I have a boyfriend . . .

T:  When you said that, the other boyfriend came to my mind, the one you left, who was someone who always knew what was the right path to keep to . . .

P:  Exactly!

. . .

P:  I am far more confident . . . I trust my choices, and this makes me feel better . . .

T:  Good.

P:  . . . because I feel that whatever I do is something I choose and I don't put up with anything I don't want, with my friends, with my parents . . . also with my mum I am much less conflicted . . . we see less of each other because I don't often return home, and she understood this . . . I am happy if they come to visit . . . and I also enjoy going to the lake at weekends . . . [change in the relationship with others/parents, different attitude to the superego]

. . .

P:  It's been a good year, I am glad . . . [loss of symptoms and of depression]

T:  So, there have not been those things that brought you here, like feeling ill?

P:  No.

T:  Like staying home, getting depressed . . .

P:  No.

T:  . . . playing the ill person . . . to get cuddles . . . [character change]

P:  [laughs] No . . . actually, not long ago, my friend Ivan . . .

T:  Friend or boyfriend?

P:  Friend . . . he said: do you realise that for a long time you have not phoned me whining and moaning . . . [character change confirmed by real-life event] True, it's been one year, not ten years . . . however, I feel well.

. . .

P:  With my mother there was a conflicted relationship, which might still be there, but I handle it differently.

T:    How did you handle it before, and how do you handle it now?

P:    Previously, I felt very hurt, and I got enraged, very much so . . . at times I let it out by consigning her to hell . . . but I recall having a lot of rage inside . . . even for minor things, such as her attitude when she complained that I never called—that was not nice of me—or that I was shitty . . . now, not that I changed or she changed . . . however . . . it doesn't hurt me so much, simply because I was able to tell her that there are many ways of giving love, and hers is not the only one and the right one . . . [change of relationship with self/other; change of relationship and different attitude with others/mother]

. . .

P:    And it was only after five years that I realised my mother regularly read my diary . . . the same as Steve, who read my emails . . . and even in that case I only realised it later on . . . and what enraged [character change] me was the delay, because if I read what I should not and discover you, my daughter, are doing something wrong, I should tell you, so that you should not make that mistake again, if I think you did wrong . . . instead, both she and Steve monitored me, waiting for me to do wrong, in order to goad me and blow it up after a lot of time had passed . . . this thing of patiently waiting until the day I can nail you . . . I think this is in the realm of sadism and of masochism for them . . . [renouncing sadomasochistic interaction: change in character pattern]

T:    With your current boyfriend this doesn't happen?

P:    No, not at all . . . with him no . . . [she has made a good enough relationship with her new partner] and he is honest, someone who listens, at the same time he is outgoing . . . if there is some problem he immediately says so . . . so even potential conflicts soften . . . it's on a day-to-day basis, and not like a build-up of things. If he is annoyed, it takes him thirty seconds to say so, and this makes me feel relaxed and I handle it better . . . so it's really different from before, also my way . . . there is a bit less passion, since with Steve there was this incredible attraction . . . with big rows and almost Hollywood-like reconciliations . . . but it was no good for me . . . at times I felt in Heaven, but it didn't last . . . this might be great for fifteen days!

. . .

T:    I'd like to know if you see a link between our work in therapy and something that happened in your life out there.

P:  It's actually . . . what I see different out there is my attitude . . . [perceives her attitude as different from before] that has really changed in many ways . . . it is more active in everything, and more determined . . . even with mistakes . . . if I make a mistake, OK: I acknowledge my mistake, because I care, but that's it . . . of course I think about it to make it different next time . . . so what I really perceive as different is my attitude.

T:  Whereas before?

P:  I did not realise!

T:  What your attitude was?

P:  It was passive . . . practically in everything . . . [is more aware of herself] . . . the difference is . . . that I learnt to know myself better, more deeply . . . and I understand what makes me feel better, and what does not . . . for instance: I fell in love with this boy [and of how the other person really is], and he is someone I would have never even considered some time ago . . . I mean, he is handsome and everything, but he doesn't have that kind of "air" I looked for—it's difficult to describe—but he is a totally different person . . . he is relaxed, calm . . . someone who would never have interested me before . . .

T:  I see, that wouldn't have attracted you before . . .

. . .

P:  Particularly with some people . . . I accepted all they told me . . . [giving up passive and subdued attitude]

T:  And with me? Didn't you happen to do the same?

P:  No, I don't think so . . . [the relationship with the therapist] nor did you ever tell me do this or do that. I don't recall having felt this, not even indirectly . . . you asked me questions, we discussed . . . at times I didn't quite understand what you were getting at, but I didn't think a lot about it . . . and [it was a corrective relational experience for the patient] at times it was like an illumination coming and, thinking of what we had discussed flashed through my mind . . . maybe a bit later, this made me think . . . but the way I experienced this path we followed . . . I believe I experienced it in a very active way. I mean— if someone asks me—what was your therapy like . . . I see it as very active, because you gave me some inputs and I probably didn't understand where I stood . . . but you gave me these inputs and were good at giving me the right ones . . .

T:  Thanks!

P:  . . . on many things, but I was capable of taking them!

T:  Certainly, you became active yourself!

P:  So . . . with you it was not the same as with my mother—to put it this way—there wasn't the same type of relationship.

T:  On the contrary.

P:  It was a very different one and, actually, OK you are a doctor and so on . . . but it brought results that I see in everyday life. That is what life is all about.

. . .

T:  Do you sometimes think of me? [exploring the real relationship with the therapist]

P:  Yes, indeed!

T:  In what frame of mind?

P:  Partly because you are very much like Peter Gabriel . . . who is my favourite singer . . . yes, I think of you. Also because now I have a friend who also started therapy, though she lost a parent and her problems are different, and sometimes she asks me, "What did he [the therapist] tell you?" . . . and of course it is a different therapy, but she goes on, "Because I really hate him! I cannot stand him! Every time I have to go I have a lump . . . did you get the same?", and I told her, "Look, there were times when I didn't feel like going, because I knew the hell that might come up and I was afraid to get shaken . . . however, I feel very warm, in that I see this person as someone who helped me . . . so . . . well I don't think of you every day, but I happen to . . . yes, yes . . . and actually, also when you asked me to come, I was glad to come and say hello.

## Concluding comments

In the course of therapy, the three corners of the triangle of conflict, reproduced above, acquired various meanings: at first, X was vital strivings, A was disapproval, D was conventional cheerfulness; then, D became submission and passive resistance; then, rage emerged in X and the other two corners were effaced; at a later stage, D was again conventional cheerfulness, hiding the desire for emotional closeness with the therapist in X, and A was disapproval again; finally, vital strivings remained in X, without any relevant D or A in operation.

At follow-up, the patient's symptoms are completely resolved, and no new symptom had taken their place. Her character has undergone deep change and her approach to all areas of life is different from before. There are signals that she is handling her life well, and managing to make progress in her affective relationships. She is grateful to the therapist, and was happy to be invited for follow-up.

## References

Abbass, A. (2002). Intensive short-term dynamic psychotherapy in a private psychiatric office. *American Journal of Psychotherapy, 56*: 225–232.

Alexander, F., & French, T. M. (1946). *Psychoanalytic Therapy, Principles and Application*. New York: Ronald Press [reprinted New York: John Wiley, 1974].

Alpert, M. (1992). Accelerated empathic therapy (AET): A new short-term dynamic psychotherapy. *International Journal of Short-Term Psychotherapy, 7*: 133–156.

American Psychiatric Association (2013). *Diagnostic and Statistical Manual of Mental Health Disorders* (5th edn). Washington, DC: American Psychiatric Association.

Bacciagaluppi, M. (1985). Inversion of parent–child relationship. A contribution to attachment theory. *British Journal of Medical Psychology, 58*: 369–373.

Bacciagaluppi, M. (1989a). The role of aggressiveness in the work of John Bowlby. *Free Associations, 16*: 123–134.

Bacciagaluppi, M. (1989b). Attachment theory as an alternative basis for psychoanalysis. *American Journal of Psychoanalysis, 49*(4): 311–318.

Bacciagaluppi, M. (1994). The relevance of attachment research to psychoanalysis and analytic social psychology. *Journal of the American Academy of Psychoanalysis, 22*: 465–479.

Bacciagaluppi, M. (2012). *Paradigms in Psychoanalysis, an Integration*. London: Karnac.

Bowlby, J. (1980). *Attachment and Loss: Vol. 3. Loss, Sadness, and Depression*. New York: Basic Books.

Bowlby, J. (1982). *Attachment and Loss: Vol 1. Attachment* (2nd edn). New York: Basic Books.

Bowlby, J. (1988). *A Secure Base*. London: Routledge.

Coughlin Della Selva, P. (1996). *Intensive Short-Term Dynamic Psychotherapy. Theory and Technique*. Chichester: John Wiley.

Davanloo, H. (1986). Intensive short-term dynamic psychotherapy with highly resistant patients. II. The course of an interview after the initial breakthrough. *International Journal of Short-Term Psychotherapy, 1*: 239–255.

Davanloo, H. (1989). The central dynamic sequence in the major unlocking of the unconscious and comprehensive trial therapy. Part II. *International Journal of Short-Term Psychotherapy, 4*: 35–66.

Davanloo, H. (1990). *Unlocking the Unconscious*. Toronto: John Wiley.

Davanloo, H. (1995). *Intensive Short-Term Dynamic Psychotherapy: Selected Papers of Habib Davanloo, MD*. Chichester: John Wiley.

Fosha, D. (Ed.) (1992). Accelerated empathic therapy (AET): history, development and theory. *International Journal of Short-Term Psychotherapy*, special issue, *7*: 3.

Fosha, D. (2000). *The Transforming Power of Affect*. New York: Basic Books.

Fosha, D. (2003). Dyadic regulation and experiential work with emotion and relatedness in trauma and disordered attachment. In: M. F. Solomon, & D. J. Siegel (Eds.), *Healing Trauma: Attachment, Trauma, the Brain and the Mind* (pp. 221–281). New York: W. W. Norton.

Fosha, D. (2009). Healing attachment trauma with attachment (and then some!). In: M. Kerman (Ed.), *Clinical Pearls of Wisdom: 21 Leading Therapists Offer their Key Insights* (pp. 43–56). New York: Norton.

Freud, S. (1923b). *The Ego and the Id. S. E., 9*: 12–59. London: Hogarth.

Freud, S. (1924c). The economic problem of masochism. *S. E., 19*: 157–170. London: Hogarth.

Kalpin, A. (2003). The use of "being present" in facilitating emotional closeness and emotional experience. *Ad Hoc Bulletin of Short-Term Dynamic Psychotherapy, 7*: 46–63.

Kalpin, A. (2008). Implementing mindfulness in experiential dynamic therapy with a depressed patient. *Ad Hoc Bulletin of Short-Term Dynamic Psychotherapy, 12*: 22–38.

Lambert, M. J., & Ogles, B. (2004). The efficacy and effectiveness of psychotherapy. In: M. J. Lambert (Ed.), *Bergin and Garfield's Handbook of Psychotherapy and Behaviour Change*. New York: Wiley.

Magnavita, J. J. (2005). *Personality Guided Relational Psychotherapy: A Unified Approach*. Washington, DC: American Psychological Association.

Main, M., & Goldwyn, R. (1998). *Adult Attachment Scoring and Classification System* (Manuscript). Berkeley, CA: University of California.

Malan, D. H. (1963). *A Study of Brief Psychotherapy*. London: Routledge, 2001.

Malan, D. H. (1976a). *The Frontier of Brief Psychotherapy*. New York: Plenum.

Malan, D. H. (1976b). *Toward the Validation of Dynamic Psychotherapy*. New York: Plenum.

Malan, D. H. (1979). *Individual Psychotherapy and the Science of Psychodynamics* (2nd edn). London: Hodder Arnold, 1995.

Malan, D. H. (1986a). Beyond interpretation: initial evaluation and technique in short-term dynamic psychotherapy. Part I. *International Journal of Short-Term Psychotherapy, 1*: 59–82.

Malan, D. H. (1986b). Beyond interpretation: initial evaluation and technique in short-term dynamic psychotherapy. Part II. *International Journal of Short-Term Psychotherapy, 1*: 83–106.

Malan, D. H., & Osimo, F. (1992). *Psychodynamics, Training, and Outcome in Brief Psychotherapy*. Oxford: Butterworth-Heinemann.

McCullough, L. (1998). Short-term psychodynamic therapy as a form of desensitization: treating affect phobias. *In session: Psychotherapy in Practice, 4*(4): 35–53.

McCullough, L. (2000). Short-term therapy for character change. In: J. Carlson & L. Sperry (Eds.), *Brief Therapy Strategies with Individuals and Couples* (pp. 127–160). New York: Zieg/Tucker.

McCullough, L., Kuhn, N., Andrews, S., Kaplan, A., Wolf, J., & Lanza-Hurley, C. (2003). *Treating Affect Phobia: A Manual for Short-Term Dynamic Psychotherapy*. New York: Guilford Press.

McCullough Vaillant, L. (1997). *Changing Character: Short-Term Anxiety-Regulating Psychotherapy for Restructuring Defenses, Affects and Attachment*. New York: Basic Books.

Neborsky, R. J. (2003). A clinical model for the comprehensive treatment of trauma using an affect experiencing-attachment theory approach. In: M. F. Solomon, & D. J. Siegel (Eds.), *Healing Trauma: Attachment, Mind, Body and Brain* (pp. 282–321). New York: W. W. Norton.

Neborsky, R. J., & Bundy, C. E. (2013). Prediction of attachment status from observation of a clinical intensive psychotherapy interview. *American Journal of Psychiatry, 67*(1): 47–71.

Osimo, F. (2001). *Parole, Emozioni e Videotape: Manuale di Psicoterapia Breve Dinamico-Esperienziale (PBDE)*. Milan: Franco Angeli.

Osimo, F. (2002). Brief psychodynamic therapy. In: J. J. Magnavita (Ed.), *Comprehensive Handbook of Psychotherapy: Psychodynamic and Object Relations Psychotherapies*. New York: Wiley.

Osimo, F. (2003). *Experiential Short-Term Dynamic Psychotherapy: A Manual.* Bloomington, IN: AuthorHouse.

Osimo, F. (2009). The character hologram. *Ad Hoc Bulletin of Short-Term Dynamic Psychotherapy: Practice and Theory, 13*: 25–50.

Osimo, F., & Stein, M. J. (2012). *Theory and Practice of Experiential Dynamic Psychotherapy.* London: Karnac.

Reich, W. (1945). *Character Analysis,* M. Boyd (Trans.). New York: Noonday Press, 1998.

Russell, E., & Fosha, D. (2008). Transformational affects and core state in AEDP: The emergence and consolidation of joy, hope, gratitude and confidence in the (solid goodness of the) self. *Journal of Psychotherapy Integration, 18*: 167–190.

Sklar, I. (1992). Issues of loss and AET. *Proceedings of the Conference: The Sequelae of Trauma.* Denville, NJ.

Svartberg, M., Stiles, T., & Seltzer, M. (2004). Randomised, controlled trial of the effectiveness of short-term dynamic psychotherapy and cognitive therapy for cluster C personality disorders. *American Journal of Psychiatry, 161*: 810–817.

ten Have-de Labije, J. (Ed.) (2001a). Red and green traffic lights on Davanloo's road to the unconscious. Part I. *The Working Alliance in ISTDP: Whose Intrapsychic Crisis?* Amsterdam: VKPD.

ten Have-de Labije, J. (2001b). Davanloo's road to the unconscious: working with a war traumatized patient and working with a phobic patient. Proceedings of the 1st IEDTA Conference, Milan. *Quaderni di Psichiatria Pratica,* special issue, 54–76.

ten Have-de Labije, J. (2010). *The Collected Writings of Josette ten Have-de Labije.* Del Mar, CA: Unlocking Press.

Tomkins, S. S. (1962). *Affect, Imagery, Consciousness: Vol. I, Positive Affects.* New York: Springer.

Tomkins, S. S. (1963). *Affect, Imagery, Consciousness: Vol. II, Negative Affects.* New York: Springer.

Wampold, B. (2001). *The Great Psychotherapy Debate: Models, Methods and Findings.* Mahwah, NJ: Lawrence Erlbaum.

Winston, A., Laikin, M., Pollack, J., Samstag, L., McCullough, L., & Muran, C. (1994). Short-term psychotherapy of personality disorders. *American Journal of Psychiatry, 151*(2): 190–194.

Winston, A., McCullough, L., Trujillo, M., Pollack, J., Laikin, M., Flegenheimer, W., & Kestenbaum, R. (1991). Brief psychotherapy of personality disorders. *Journal of Nervous and Mental Disease, 179*(4): 188–193.

# Concluding remarks

*Marco Bacciagaluppi*

The interest of this book lies chiefly in the unpublished material by John Bowlby: the excerpts from his correspondence with me, and the Milan seminar, in which he presents his theoretical views and then discusses three case histories, in addition to other circumscribed topics.

In the correspondence, he reveals sharp attention to new developments, such as Greenberg and Mitchell's book, and great readiness to share his knowledge and give advice, from which I greatly benefited. I believe he was moved when I discovered the pre-war book he had written with his friend Evan Durbin, who later died prematurely. The longest letter he wrote to me was about his friend. One characteristic that stands out in the correspondence is Bowlby's constant involvement with the USA. As he states in the Acknowledgments in *Attachment*, his work at the Tavistock had been supported by American Foundations, and he had been to Stanford on a fellowship and later as Visiting Professor. In his correspondence with me, he repeatedly apologises for answering late on account of lecture tours in the USA, in particular at neo-Freudian institutions such as the William Alanson White Society and the Karen Horney Psychoanalytic Institute (where he presented "Violence in the family"), which he obviously found very congenial. When I asked him who else was moving in the same direction as he, he mentioned five American authors (letter of 24th June, 1982).

After the theoretical introduction, in the rest of the seminar we have the opportunity to see Bowlby at work at a clinical level. He is revealed as a very warm person: he expresses appreciation of each of the therapists presenting cases, sympathy for the difficulty of their work, and empathy with the patients presented. The three presentations by Leopolda Pelizzaro, Ferruccio Osimo, and Emilia Fumagalli all reveal a deep commitment on the part of the therapist, which Bowlby acknowledged in all three cases.

Bowlby specifically shows his gift as a clinician in his misgivings concerning Milly's patient, which were unfortunately confirmed, and in the detection of the inverted relationship established by Leopolda's patient with her daughter. If I may add a comment of my own, in the case of Leopolda's patient there was a transgenerational transmission of an inverted relationship, because the patient had been expected to cheer up her parents. A further example of Bowlby's insight as a clinician is his discussion of the second dream of Ferruccio's patient, which reveals the presence of a battering mother, who was otherwise absent from the patient's communications, and his hypothesis that the patient's elder sister might have been a mother substitute. As Milly states in her report, her patient is a very tragic example of Bowlby's principle that, if an attachment figure is threatening, the child clings all the more.

Claudia's report is a very moving account of the encounter with the Bowlbys as a human, as well as a scientific, experience, because it coincided with her first pregnancy, and when the baby was born the Bowlbys sent her a gift.

In addition to amusing incidents concerning Bowlby's and his wife's stay in Milan, with the charming detail of the gift of a book by Beatrix Potter to their little son Guido, the scientific contribution of Germana Agnetti and Angelo Barbato consists chiefly of an integration of attachment theory and systemic family therapy, thus linking two important traditions that had hitherto remained disconnected. In this regard, they call attention to an early paper by Bowlby on group tension in the family. An example of the political radicalism mentioned by them as characterising the 1970s in Italy is provided by Leopolda's patient, who joined a revolutionary group.

Ferruccio Osimo's contribution is a tribute to the fruitfulness of attachment theory. It influenced not only his own work, but also that of many others in the field of brief psychotherapy, as he states in his report. I believe that in his own case his orientation was decisively influenced by his personal encounter with Bowlby at the seminar.

In the long case report in his contribution, he shows how he unceasingly works on the patient's defences, displayed in mood and posture, in order to bring out the underlying feelings. In using the brief therapy format, he was influenced by his training with Malan at the Tavistock, prior to the seminar, while, in his attack on defences, he was influenced by his training with Davanloo, subsequent to the seminar, and ultimately by Wilhelm Reich's *Character Analysis* (Reich, 1949).

These approaches are all anticipated by Bowlby in what is possibly his most specific contribution to therapy, Lecture 8 in *A Secure Base* (Bowlby, 1988), titled "Attachment, communication, and the therapeutic process", which was based on an earlier paper of 1977. In this paper, he lists "the three principal forms of analytic psychotherapy in use today – individual therapy, family therapy, and group therapy" (p. 138). In turn, individual psychotherapy can be short-term or long-term. In connection with short-term therapy, on page 140, he quotes Malan (1973). He then lists five therapeutic tasks: (1) to provide a secure base; (2) to examine the patient's current relationships outside therapy; (3) to do the same with the current relationship with the therapist; (4) to examine links between current relationships and past relationships; and (5), finally, to explore alternative possibilities of relationship. Points 2, 3, and 4 are the three vertices, or corners, of Malan's triangle of persons, which is systematically utilised by Osimo (Malan & Osimo, 1992). In the section on "The therapist's stance" (p. 151), Bowlby points out the need for activity on the therapist's part. Finally, in the last section (p. 154), Bowlby stresses the importance of emotional communication between therapist and patient. "There are, in fact, no more important communications between one human being and another than those expressed emotionally" (p. 156). This is the concluding sentence of the lecture: "It is the emotional communications between a patient and his therapist that play the crucial part" (p. 157). Another point on which Bowlby concurs with Ferruccio is the usefulness of long sessions, which Bowlby mentions in the seminar.

One point I would stress in the follow-up interview with Ferruccio's patient is the expression of a new emotion: gratitude. I suggest that this is the same emotion that impelled Bowlby to write his book on Darwin: out of gratitude for the powerful theory that Darwin had provided, he reciprocated with concern for Darwin's ill-health (Bowlby, 1990).

I believe all this shows that Ferruccio Osimo is following in the footsteps of John Bowlby. Ultimately, any approach that includes the intense involvement of the therapist goes back to that great pioneer, Ferenczi (1933).

## References

Bowlby, J. (1988). *A Secure Base*. London: Routledge.

Bowlby, J. (1990). *Charles Darwin. A Biography*. London: Hutchinson.

Ferenczi, S. (1933). Confusion of tongues between adults and the child. In: S. Ferenczi (1955). *Final Contributions to the Problems and Methods of Psycho-Analysis*. London: Maresfield Reprints, 1980.

Malan, D. H. (1973). Therapeutic factors in analytically-oriented brief psychotherapy. In: R. H. Gosling (Ed.), *Support, Innovation and Autonomy*, 187–209. London: Tavistock.

Malan, D. H., & Osimo, F. (1992). *Psychodynamics, Training, and Outcome in Brief Psychotherapy*. Oxford: Butterworth-Heinemann.

Reich, W. (1949). *Character Analysis* (3rd edn). New York: Noonday Press.

# INDEX

For Product Safety Concerns and Information please contact our EU
representative  GPSR@taylorandfrancis.com
Taylor & Francis Verlag GmbH, Kaufingerstraße 24, 80331 München, Germany